Lecture Notes in Computer Science

Commenced Publication in 1973
Founding and Former Series Editors:
Gerhard Goos, Juris Hartmanis, and Jan van Leeuwen

Jean-Marc Pierson (Ed.)

Data Management in Grids

First VLDB Workshop, DMG 2005
Trondheim, Norway, September 2-3, 2005
Revised Selected Papers

 Springer

Volume Editor

Jean-Marc Pierson
Lyon Research Center for Images and Intelligent Information Systems (LIRIS)
National Institute of Applied Science (INSA de Lyon)
69631 Villeurbanne, France
E-mail: jean-marc.pierson@liris.cnrs.fr

Library of Congress Control Number: 2005938219

CR Subject Classification (1998): H.2, H.4, H.3, H.2.4, E.2, H.5, C.2

ISSN   0302-9743
ISBN-10   3-540-31212-9 Springer Berlin Heidelberg New York
ISBN-13   978-3-540-31212-3 Springer Berlin Heidelberg New York

Springer is a part of Springer Science+Business Media

springer.com

Typesetting: Camera-ready by author, data conversion by Scientific Publishing Services, Chennai, India
Printed on acid-free paper   SPIN: 11611950   06/3142   5 4 3 2 1 0

Message from the Program Chair

It was my great pleasure to welcome you in Trondheim for the first "Data Management in Grids" workshop, associated to the VLDB conference. Since the mid-1990s and the emergence of Grids, many research activities have been initiated in relation to data management in these dynamic, heterogeneous and cross-organizational environments. The database community can offer its unique expertise in the management of very large, widely distributed databases. Conversely, Grids offer a novel and very exciting field of research for database scientists both in terms of application domains and fundamental research.

This workshop was intended to bring together these two communities, and thus to offer a unique workspace for researchers to discuss and exchange ideas about the emerging challenges and opportunities offered by Data Grids. The co-location with the VLDB conference attracted researchers from both fields and launched interesting discussions.

The call for papers attracted 24 submissions. From the submissions, the Program Committee selected nine regular papers for the one-day workshop. The international flavor (seven countries represented for the final program) produced a very enriching and interactive workshop. In addition to the paper presentations, the program also included two invited talks : "Globally Distributed Data" by Reagan Moore, San Diego Super-computing Center, USA, and "An Outline of the Global Grid Forum Data Access and Integration Service Specifications," by Mario Antonioletti, University of Edinburgh, UK.

I would like to thank all those who submitted papers for consideration, the participants of the conference, and the members of the Program Committee for their hard and conscientious work, their time and their careful effort in the reviewing process.

2005   Jean-Marc Pierson

Organization

Program Chair
Jean-Marc Pierson, LIRIS, INSA-Lyon, France

Program Committee
Lionel Brunie, LIRIS, France
Rajkumar Buyya, University of Melbourne, Australia
Neil P. Chue Hong, EPCC, The University of Edinburgh, UK
Alvaro A.A. Fernandes, The University of Manchester, UK
Ian Foster, Argone National Laboratory, USA
Dieter Gawlick, Oracle, USA
Peter Kacsuk, Mta Sztaki Research Institute, Hungary
Peter Kunszt, CERN, Switzerland
Stephen A. Langella, The Ohio State University, USA
Susan Malaika, IBM, USA
Johan Montagnat, CNRS, France
Reagan Moore, SDSC, USA
Gianluca Moro, DEIS - University of Bologna, Italy
Brigitte Plateau, ID-IMAG, France
Thierry Priol, IRISA, France
Heinz Stockinger, University of Vienna, Austria

External Reviewers
Gabriel Antoniu
Yves Denneulin
Sushant Goel
Yvon Jégou
Fabrice Jouanot
Stefano Lodi
Gabriele Monti
Ludwig Seitz
Olivier Valentin
Christine Verdier

Table of Contents

Globally Distributed Data
  Reagan W. Moore.. 1

XML Data Integration in OGSA Grids
  Carmela Comito, Domenico Talia............................... 4

Towards Dynamic Information Integration
  Jürgen Göres.. 16

Adapting to Changing Resource Performance in Grid Query
Processing
  Anastasios Gounaris, Jim Smith, Norman W. Paton,
  Rizos Sakellariou, Alvaro A.A. Fernandes, Paul Watson 30

An Adaptive Distributed Query Processing Grid Service
  Fabio Porto, Vinícius F.V. da Silva, Márcio L. Dutra,
  Bruno Schulze... 45

Framework for Querying Distributed Objects Managed by a Grid
Infrastructure
  Ruslan Fomkin, Tore Risch 58

An Outline of the Global Grid Forum Data Access and Integration
Service Specifications
  Mario Antonioletti, Amy Krause, Norman W. Paton 71

File Caching in Data Intensive Scientific Applications on
Data-Grids
  Ekow Otoo, Doron Rotem, Alexandru Romosan,
  Sridhar Seshadri.. 85

RRS: Replica Registration Service for Data Grids
  Arie Shoshani, Alex Sim, Kurt Stockinger....................... 100

Datagridflows: Managing Long-Run Processes on Datagrids
  Arun Jagatheesan, Jonathan Weinberg, Reena Mathew, Allen Ding,
  Erik Vandekieft, Daniel Moore, Reagan Moore, Lucas Gilbert,
  Mark Tran, Jeffrey Kuramoto 113

Servicing Seismic and Oil Reservoir Simulation Data Through Grid
Data Services
Sivaramakrishnan Narayanan, Tahsin Kurc, Umit Catalyurek,
Joel Saltz 129

Author Index 143

Globally Distributed Data

Reagan W. Moore

San Diego Supercomputer Center,
San Diego, CA
moore@sdsc.edu

The management of globally distributed data is simplified through the use of data grids which enable data sharing environments. Data grids provide both the interoperability mechanisms needed to interact with legacy storage systems and legacy applications, as well as the logical name spaces needed to identify files, resources, and users. Data grids also provide support for consistent management of state information about each file within the distributed environment. The state information includes access controls, descriptive metadata, and administration metadata. These capabilities enable data virtualization, the ability to manage data independently of the chosen storage repositories. Applications that manage globally distributed data include data grid federations, distributed digital libraries, and distributed persistent archives.

The Storage Resource Broker (SRB), developed at the San Diego Supercomputer Center, is an example of generic data grid software infrastructure that uses database technology to manage state information for globally shared collections. The software has been under development since 1995, initially funded by the Defense Advanced Research Project Agency to support Massive Data Analysis Systems. Subsequent projects focused on the application of the technology in support of distributed data management. Across most of the projects that use data grid technology, the goal of distributed data management was either:

- sharing of data. Scientists share original data sets while pursuing research.
- publication of data. Scientists register data sets used in the research into a digital library for future discovery and access.
- preservation of data. This corresponds to the creation of standard digital reference sets that are then used as the intellectual capital of the discipline. New theory or observational results are compared against these reference data. The technology that manages infrastructure independence (ability to migrate collections onto new hardware and software systems) is called a persistent archive.

The application areas included a patent digital library for the US Patent and Trademark Office; Department of Energy high energy physics data grids; prototype research persistent archives for the National Archives and Records Administration; National Library of Medicine digital library for digital embryo images; National Science Foundation persistent archive for the National Science Digital Library; National Institute of Health Biomedical Informatics Research Network data grid for neuroscience data; NSF Real-time Observatories, Applications, and Data Management network for sensor data; and NSF National Virtual Observatory for astronomy sky surveys.

J.-M. Pierson (Ed.): VLDB DMG 2005, LNCS 3836, pp. 1–3, 2005.
© Springer-Verlag Berlin Heidelberg 2005

Each project defined standard descriptive metadata, standard data encoding formats, and standard services that would be used to manipulate the data. The descriptive metadata were organized in a collection hierarchy along with administrative metadata that represented state information managed by the data grid. Data grids separated the management of the state information from the storage of the data. The result of each operation on the material within the data grid was tracked and the associated state information was associated with the files that were manipulated. An example is the creation of a replica of a file. The location of the replica and the date it was created were registered into a metadata catalog that is maintained in a relational database.

A typical project assembled a shared collection that contained 1-million to 2-million files, with the largest shared collection holding over 27 million files. The sizes of the collections ranged from 1-2 terabytes to collections of simulation data that exceeded 150 terabytes. The collections were organized by groups of researchers that contained 20 persons up to several hundred persons.

SDSC is approaching the issue of global data management from three different perspectives:

1. Data virtualization: Create a shared collection that manages the name spaces for resources, files, users, metadata, and access controls independently from the storage system.
2. Access virtualization: Integrate distributed data management into major applications such as digital libraries, persistent archives, and real-time sensor data management systems.
3. State information virtualization: Define the consistency constraints that are applied in the update of state information, and provide the ability to change the constraints when federating data grids, modifying views of collections, managing data placement, or asserting global consistency properties.

The data virtualization efforts are exemplified through the use of the SRB to manage logical name spaces to provide persistent global naming. In addition, the SRB differentiates between the access methods required by preferred interfaces, and the storage repository protocols required to interact with legacy storage systems. The SRB maps from the access interface protocol to a standard set of operations for manipulating data and metadata. The SRB then maps from a standard set of operations that will be performed at a storage repository to the particular protocol required by that system. The result is the ability to manage data that is distributed across multiple types of storage systems, while providing a uniform access interface.

The access virtualization builds upon the data virtualization through the integration of advanced user interfaces. A major example is the integration of digital library technology with data grid technology. The goal is the ability to provide digital library services on collections that are distributed across multiple storage systems, and authentication domains.

An example is the integration of the DSpace digital library, developed at MIT and Hewelett Packard, with the Storage Resource Broker data grid. The resulting system is able to support:

- creation of DSpace collections whose size is greater than the local disk capacity
- replication of digital entities between sites for disaster recovery
- access to digital entities that reside in another DSpace instance

A similar effort is being done to integrate the Fedora digital library, developed at University of Virginia and Cornell University, on top of the Storage Resource Broker data grid.

The state information virtualization is a new research effort with the goal of producing the next generation of data management technology. When federating data grids that manage different consistency constraints, the ability to characterize the chosen constraints becomes important. Building a shared collection that crosses multiple environments with different consistency requirements can be accomplished through the direct association of the governing constraint with each metadata attribute. Two types of constraints are required: procedural rules that are followed when state information is updated, and global consistency constraints that can be verified as properties of a sub-collection. This latter example is one of the major challenges of distributed data management systems, namely how to create consistent state from possibly inconsistent state.

For further information, see http://www.sdsc.edu/srb.

XML Data Integration in OGSA Grids

Carmela Comito and Domenico Talia

DEIS, University of Calabria,
Via P. Bucci 41 c,
87036 Rende, Italy
{ccomito, talia}@deis.unical.it
http://www.deis.unical.it/

Abstract. Data integration is the flexible and managed federation, analysis, and processing of data from different distributed sources. Data integration is becoming as important as data mining for exploiting the value of large and distributed data sets that are available today. Distributed processing infrastructures such as Grids can be used for data integration on geographically distributed sites. This paper presents a framework for integrating heterogeneous XML data sources distributed among the nodes of a Grid. We propose a query reformulation algorithm to combine and query XML documents through a decentralized point-to-point mediation process among the different data sources based on schema mappings. The above cited XML integration formalism is exposed as a Grid Service within the GDIS architecture. GDIS is a service-based architecture for providing data integration in Grids using a decentralized approach. The underlying model of such architecture is discussed and we show how it fits the XMAP formalism/algorithm.

1 Introduction

The Grid offers new opportunities and raises new challenges in data management arising from large scale, dynamic, autonomous, and distributed nature of data sources. A Grid can include related data resources maintained in different syntaxes, managed by different software systems, and accessible through different protocols and interfaces. Due to this diversity in data resources, one of the most demanding issue in managing data on Grids is reconciliation of data heterogeneity. Therefore, in order to provide facilities for addressing requests over multiple heterogeneous data sources, it is necessary to provide data integration models and mechanisms.

Data integration is the flexible and managed federation, analysis, and processing of data from different distributed sources. In particular, the rise in availability of web-based data sources has led new challenges in data integration systems for obtaining decentralized, wide-scale sharing of data, preserving semantics. These new needs in data integration systems are also felt in Grid settings. In a Grid it is not suitable to refer to a centralized structure for coordinating all the nodes because it can become a bottleneck and, most of all, it doesn't benefit from the dynamic and distributed nature of Grid resources.

The Grid community is devoting great attention toward the management of structured and semi-structured data such as databases and XML data. The most

J.-M. Pierson (Ed.): VLDB DMG 2005, LNCS 3836, pp. 4–15, 2005.

significant examples of such efforts are the *OGSA Data Access and Integration* (OGSA-DAI) [1] and the *OGSA Distributed Query Processor* (OGSA-DQP) [2] projects. However, till today only few of those projects [3,4] actually meet schema-integration issues necessary for establishing semantic connections among heterogeneous data sources.

For these reasons, we propose a framework for integrating heterogeneous XML data sources distributed over a Grid. By designing this framework, we aim at developing a decentralized network of semantically related schemas that enables the formulation of distributed queries over heterogeneous data sources. We designed a method to combine and query XML documents through a decentralized point-to-point mediation process among the different data sources based on schema mappings. We offer a decentralized service-based architecture that exposes this XML integration formalism as a Grid Service [5]. We refer to this architecture as the *Grid Data Integration System* (GDIS). The GDIS infrastructure exploits the middleware provided by OGSA-DQP, OGSA-DAI, and Globus Toolkit 3 [6], building on top of them schema-integration services.

The remainder of the paper is organized as follows. Section 2 presents a short analysis of data integration systems focusing on specific issues related to Grids. Section 3 presents the XMAP integration framework; the underlying integration model and the XMAP query reformulation algorithm are described. Section 4 illustrates the deployment of the XMAP framework on a service-based Grid architecture. Finally, Section 5 outlines future work and draws some conclusions.

2   Data Integration and Grids

The goal of a data integration system is to combine heterogeneous data residing at different sites by providing a unified view of this data. The two main approaches to data integration are federated database management systems (FDBMSs) and traditional mediator/wrapper-based integration systems.

A federated database management system (FDBMS) [7] is a collection of co-operating but autonomous component database systems (DBSs). The DBMS of a component DBS, or component DBMS, can be a centralized or distributed DBMS or another FDBMS. The component DBMSs can differ in different aspects such as data models, query languages, and transaction management capabilities.

Traditional data integration systems [8] are characterized by an architecture based on one or more mediated schemas and a set of sources. The sources contain the real data, while every mediated schema provides a reconciled, integrated, and virtual view of the underlying sources. Moreover, the system includes a set of source descriptions that provide semantic mappings between the relations in the source schemas and the relations in the mediated schemas [9].

Data integration on Grids presents a twofold characterization:

1. data integration is a key issue for exploiting the availability of large, heterogeneous, distributed and highly dynamic data volumes on Grids;
2. integration formalisms can benefit from an OGSA-based Grid infrastructure, since it facilitates dynamic discovery, allocation, access, and use of both data

sources and computational resources, as required to support computationally demanding database operations such as query reformulation, compilation and evaluation.

Data integration on Grids has to deal with unpredictable, highly dynamic data volumes provided by unpredictable membership of nodes that happen to be participating at any given time. So, traditional approaches to data integration, such as FDBMS [7] and the use of mediator/wrapper middleware [9], are not suitable in Grid settings. The federation approach is a rather rigid configuration where resources allocation is static and optimization cannot take advantage of evolving circumstances in the execution environment. The design of mediator/wrapper integration systems must be done globally and the coordination of mediators has to be done centrally, which is an obstacle to the exploitation of evolving characteristics of dynamic environments. As a consequence, data sources cannot change often and significantly, otherwise they may violate the mappings to the mediated schema.

The rise in availability of web-based data sources has led to new challenges in data integration systems in order to obtain decentralized, wide-scale sharing of semantically-related data. Recently, several works on data management in peer-to-peer (P2P) systems are moving along this direction [10, 11, 12, 13]. All these systems focus on an integration approach not based on a global schema: each peer represents an autonomous information system, and data integration is achieved by establishing mappings among the various peers.

To the best of our knowledge, there are only few works designed to provide schema-integration in Grids. The most notable ones are *Hyper* [3] and *GDMS* [4]. Both systems are based on the same approach that we have used ourselves: building data integration services by extending the reference implementation of OGSA-DAI. The *Grid Data Mediation Service* (GDMS) uses a wrapper/mediator approach based on a global schema. GDMS presents heterogeneous, distributed data sources as one logical virtual data source in the form of an OGSA-DAI service. This work is essentially different from ours as it uses a global schema. For its part, *Hyper* is a framework that integrates relational data in P2P systems built on Grid infrastructures. As in other P2P integration systems, the integration is achieved without using any hierarchical structure for establishing mappings among the autonomous peers. In that framework, the authors use a simple relational language for expressing both the schemas and the mappings. By comparison, our integration model follows as Hyper an approach not based on a hierarchical structure, however differently from Hyper it focuses on XML data sources and is based on schema-mappings that associate paths in different schemas.

3   A Decentralized XML Data Integration Framework

In this section, we describe a framework meant to integrate heterogeneous XML data sources distributed among nodes of a Grid. The primary design goal of this framework is to develop a decentralized network of semantically related schemas that enables the formulation of queries over heterogeneous, distributed data sources.

The environment is modeled as a system composed of a number of Grid nodes, where each node can hold one or more XML databases. These nodes are connected to each other through declarative mappings rules. The framework implements then a method to combine and query XML documents through a decentralized point-to-point mediation process among the different data sources. Moreover, the interface it exposes to access and query the XML data sources is completely uniform, regardless of the intrinsic complexity of the underlying system.

3.1   Integration Model

Our integration model is based on schema mappings to translate queries between different schemas. The goal of a schema mapping is to capture structural as well as terminological correspondences between schemas.

As mentioned before, traditional centralized architecture of data integration systems is not suitable for highly dynamic and distributed environments such as the Grid. Thus, we propose an approach inspired from [13] where the mapping rules are established directly among source schemas without relying on a central mediator or a hierarchy of mediators. In consequence, in our integration model, there is no global schema representing all data sources in a unique data model but a collection of local schemas (the native schema of each data source). This way, the coordination of the various nodes is completely decentralized. Each node is free to establish the semantic connections with the source schemas it considers more appropriate. Therefore, to integrate a source in the system, one needs only to provide a set of mapping rules that describes the relationships between its schema and the other schemas it is related to.

The specification of mappings is thus flexible and scalable. Regardless of the total number of nodes composing the system, each source schema is directly connected to only a small number of other schemas. However, it remains reachable from all other schemas that belong to its "transitive closure". For any mapping M, its closure is defined as the set of rules that can be derived from M by repeated composition of schema paths. In other words, the system supports two different kinds of mapping to connect schemas semantically: *point-to-point* mappings and *transitive* mappings. In transitive mappings, data sources are related through one or more "mediator schemas". For example, if we have a source A directly connected to a source B and B connected to C, A is connected to *both* B and C. Establishing the mappings this way creates a graph of semantically related sources where each of the sources knows its direct semantic neighbors (point-to-point mapping) and can learn about the mappings of its neighbors (transitive mapping). Therefore, in our integration model all nodes are equal: there is no distinction between data sources and mediators. Each node acts both as a data source contributing data and as a local mediator providing an uniform view over the data provided by other nodes.

We address structural heterogeneity among XML data sources by associating paths in different schemas. Mappings are specified as path expressions that relate a specific element or attribute (together with its path) in the source schema to related elements or attributes in the destination schema. The data integration model we propose is indeed based on path-to-path mappings expressed in the XPath [14] query language, assuming XML Schema as the data model for XML sources. Specifically, this means that a path in a source is described in terms of XPath expressions.

As a first step, we consider only a subset of the full XPath language. The expressions of such a fragment of XPath are given by the following grammar:

$$q \to n \mid . \mid q \,/\, q \mid q \,//\, q \mid q \,[\, q \,]$$

where "n" is any label (node tests), "." denotes the "current node", "/" indicates the child axis (/) whereas "//" the descendant axis, and "[ ]" denotes a predicate.

A schema mapping is defined as a set of "formulas" that relate a pair of schemas. More precisely, we define a mapping M over a source schema S as a set of mapping rules $\mathcal{R}^M = \{R_1^M, R_2^M, \ldots R_k^M\}$. As we perform path-to-path mappings, a mapping rule associates paths in different schemas. Specifically, a mapping rule is an expression of the form:

$$R^M : \{S_S, P_S\} \longrightarrow_{C^M} \{S_D, P_D^+\}, \text{ where:}$$

- R^M is the label of the rule.
- S_S is the source schema with respect to which the rules are established.
- P_S is a path expression in the source schema.
- S_D is the target schema with respect to which the semantic connections are established.
- P_D is a path expression in the destination schema (the cardinality of this element may be more than one).
- C^M is the element denoting the cardinality of the mappings between the two schemas. Mappings are classified as 1-1, 1-N, N-1, N-N according to the number of nodes (both elements and attributes) of the schemas involved in the mapping relationship. Before characterizing the cardinality constraints, one should note that the paths involved in the mappings are "terminal" paths. By terminal paths we mean paths whose leaf nodes are terminal elements or attributes. 1-1 mappings state that there exist an univocal correspondence between the source element and the destination one. In 1-N mappings (one-element to many-elements) there is a component (attribute or element) represented by one element in the source schema but by many elements in the destination schema. In N-1 mappings (many-elements to one-element) more than one node in the source schema corresponds to one node in the destination schema. We have chosen, for the sake of complexity, not to consider N-N mappings (many-elements to many-elements) in this model.

The mapping rules are specified in XML documents called XMAP documents. Each source schema in the framework is associated to an XMAP document containing all the mapping rules related to it.

The structure of XMAP documents is conform to the schema shown in Figure 1. One can notice the presence of a single sourceSchema element, and a set of Rule elements defining the mapping rules. Rule elements have a complex structure which specifies the paths involved in the mappings and the cardinality constraints among them.

```
<schema targetNamespace="http://XMAP/XMAPDocument"
        xmlns="http://www.w3.org/2001/XMLSchema" ?>
 <element name="Mapping">
  <complexType>
   <sequence>
    <element name="sourceSchema" type="string"
             minOccurs="1" maxOccurs="1"/>
    <element name="Rule" minOccurs="1">
     <complexType>
      <sequence>
       <attribute name="Cardinality" type="string"
                  minOccurs="1" maxOccurs="1"/>
       <element name="sourcePath" type="string" minOccurs="1"/>
       <element name="destSchema" type="string"
                minOccurs="1" maxOccurs="1"/>
       <element name="destPath" type="string" minOccurs="1"/>
      </sequence>
     </complexType>
    </element>
   </sequence>
  </complexType>
 </element>
</schema>
```

Fig. 1. XML schema for XMAP documents

3.2   A Reformulation Algorithm for XPath Queries

In this section we present an algorithm to reformulate an XPath query on the basis of the mapping rules established for the schema over which the query is formulated. In the following, we suppose that we have a set of XML data sources, that each data source is compliant to an XML Schema and that, for each schema, an XMAP document containing the mappings related to this schema is provided.

Our query processing approach exploits the semantic connections established in the system by performing the *query reformulation algorithm* before executing the query, in order to gain further knowledge. This way, when a query is posed over the schema of a source, the system will be able to use data from any source that is transitively connected by semantic mappings. Indeed, it will reformulate the given query expanding and translating it into appropriate queries for each semantically related source. Thus, the user can retrieve data from all the related sources in the system by simply submitting a single XPath query.

Differently from many integration approaches, where the partial query results from different sources are joined to obtain the overall query result, we allow for partial query answering, in the sense that the response to a query is provided by each source independently. This way, we don't have to wait (for a period which might be rather important) the end of the execution of all the queries in which the original query has been reformulated.

As stated previously, schema mappings associate paths in different schemas, so reformulating a query with a mapping rule means replacing its paths with the corresponding ones. Obviously enough, this "replacement" is not just a simple substitution, and the mapping rule establishes how and under which constraints it is possible to do such a transformation. More precisely, the proposed algorithm exploits path-to-path mappings and focuses on how to take advantage of schema semantics to generate consistent translations from the source to the target by considering the constraints and the structure of the target schema. The query reformulation algorithm uses as input an XPath query and the mappings, and it produces as output zero, one or more reformulated queries. We describe now in details the logic of the algorithm. In this discussion, we use Q to denote the input XPath query, S the source schema over which Q is formulated, M the mappings in the system and Q_{R_i} the reformulated queries produced by the algorithm.

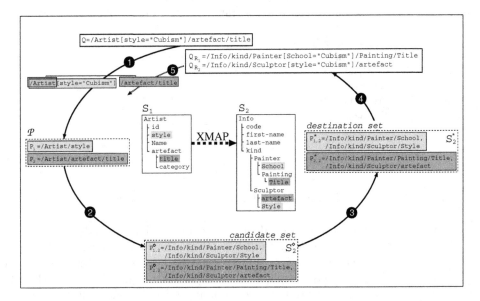

Fig. 2. Example of use of the XMAP algorithm

The algorithm can be decomposed in the following stages:

1. *Identifying the path expressions* in Q.
   An XPath query can contain one or more predicates that produce different branching points in the tree pattern representing the query. Each of these branches identifies a specific path in the XML data source. The paths identified in the query are collected into a set $\mathcal{P}$.
2. *Looking for candidate paths in all source schemas related to S.*
   The goal of this stage is to find corresponding paths in all sources semantically related to S. This means finding the path expressions corresponding to every element P_i in $\mathcal{P}$, by using the mapping information specified in the XMAP document provided with S. More precisely, for each P_i of the query Q, the

algorithm looks for all corresponding paths in the schemas transitively connected to S through path P_i. These paths $P_{i,j}^\diamond$ are called *candidate paths*, and the schema $S_j^\diamond$ they belong to, *candidate schema*. In particular we define a *candidate element* $E_{i,j}^\diamond$ as a tuple $\langle S_j^\diamond, \{P_{i,j}^\diamond\}\rangle$, where $\{P_{i,j}^\diamond\}$ is a set of paths over the schema $S_j^\diamond$. So, for each path expression $P_i \in \mathcal{P}$, zero, one or more candidate elements $E_{i,j}^\diamond$ are built with $0 \leq j \leq n$ (n is the number of source schemas in the system). A *candidate set* $\mathcal{E}^\diamond$ is a set of candidate elements $\{E_1^\diamond, \ldots E_n^\diamond\}$ (with $E_j^\diamond = \bigcup_i E_{i,j}^\diamond$). This stage returns as a result the set $\mathcal{E}^\diamond$.

3. *Pruning of candidate schemas.*
The third stage of the algorithm checks for each candidate schema found in the previous stage whether it may be used to obtain one or more reformulation of the query Q. To this aim, the algorithm checks whether each candidate schema has at least one candidate path for each path present in the query. Moreover, it needs to make sure that none of these candidate paths has already been used to rewrite Q in order to avoid considering redundant paths. The schemas that meet both these conditions are the only ones that we will be considered to obtain reformulated queries, we call them destination schemas. We define a *destination element* $E_{i,j}^\star$ as a tuple $\langle S_j^\star, \{P_{i,j}^\star\}\rangle$, where $\{P_{i,j}^\star\}$ is a set of paths over the schema $S_j^\star$. So, for each path expression P_i in $\mathcal{P}$, zero, one or more candidate elements $E_{i,j}^\star$ are built where $0 \leq j \leq |\mathcal{E}^\diamond|$. A *destination set* $\mathcal{E}^\star$ is a set of destination elements $\{E_1^\star, \ldots E_n^\star\}$ (with $E_j^\star = \bigcup_i E_{i,j}^\star$). Thus, this stage returns as a result the set $\mathcal{E}^\star$.

4. *Constructing reformulated queries.*
In this stage, given the set $\mathcal{E}^\star$, the algorithm produces one or more XPath queries over each schema in the set. More precisely, for each destination schema $S_j^\star$ in $\mathcal{E}^\star$ the following steps are performed:

   - *Assessing cardinality constraints.* If each path P_i in $\mathcal{P}$ has a single correspondent path $P_{i,j}^\star$ in the schema $S_j^\star$, all the mapping rules between S and $S_j^\star$ will be of kind 1-1 or N-1. Thus, the output of the reformulation will be a single query expressed over the destination schema $S_j^\star$. At the opposite, if there exists (at least) one path in $\mathcal{P}$ that has more than one destination path over the schema $S_j^\star$ (1-N mapping), there will be more than one reformulated query over the schema $S_j^\star$. The number of reformulated queries depends on the possible path combinations. If k is the cardinality of the set $\mathcal{P}$, $|\mathcal{P}|$, the number *com* of possible distinct path combinations for $S_j^\star$, is equal to the product of the cardinality of each path $P_{i,j}^\star$, $com = |P_{1,j}^\star| \times |P_{2,j}^\star| \times \cdots \times |P_{k,j}^\star|$.
   - *Checking Join conditions.* Once the cardinality of the mapping has been established, and before actually producing the query, one needs to check the join conditions between the paths $P_{i,j}^\star (1 \leq i \leq |\mathcal{P}|)$ of the destination schema $S_j^\star$. In the 1-1 and N-1 mapping cases, since there will be a single reformulated query, it will not be possible to reformulate the query with respect to the schema $S_j^\star$ if there exist at least two paths for which join conditions are not respected. Finally, in the 1-N mapping case, there will be as many reformulated queries as there exist satisfied join conditions among the paths of each combination.

- *Composing XPath Queries.* Once the join conditions between the destination paths have been checked, the actual production of one or more XPath queries is initiated. These queries are the product of the reformulation of the query Q in the destination schema $S_j^\star$.

5. *Recursive invocation of the algorithm.*
   The algorithm is recursively invoked over the reformulated queries in order to produce the queries corresponding to every transitive mappings.

In Figure 2 is described an example of use of the XMAP algorithm. Here a query Q is formulated over the schema S_1. In the first step the algorithm identifies the paths P_1 and P_2 in Q and produces as output the set $\mathcal{P}$. Next, exploiting the XMAP document associated to the schema S_1, the algorithm finds two mapping rules connecting S_1 to S_2 trough the paths P_1 and P_2. More precisely, one of these rules relates P1 to two paths in S_2, respectively /Info/kind/Painter/School and /Info/Kind/Sculptor/Artefact. Similarly, the other mapping rules relates P_2 to /Info/Kind/Painter/Painting/Title and /Info/Kind/Sculptor/artefact. So, the second step of the algorithm produces as output a candidate set composed of the elements $P_{i,j}^\diamond$ and the (candidate) schema $S_2^\diamond$. In the considered example as the schema $S_2^\diamond$ has correspondences for both paths P_1 and P_2, it is identified as a destination schema (step 3), so it can be used to reformulate the query Q. In particular, the algorithm produces two reformulations of the query Q over the schema S_2, respectively Q_{R_1} and Q_{R_2}.

In Figure 3 is shown the pseudo-code of the XMAP reformulation algorithm.

Algorithm QueryReformulation
Input: query Q, schema S, mapping M (M is the XMAP of S)
Output: set of reformulated queries $\mathcal{Q}^\star$

---

begin
    $\mathcal{P} \leftarrow$ IdentifyPath(Q);
    for each path $P_i \in \mathcal{P}$ do
        $\mathcal{E}^\diamond \leftarrow$ FindCandidatePath(P_i, M);
    $\mathcal{E}^\star \leftarrow$ PruningSchema($\mathcal{E}^\diamond$);
    for each $S_j^\star \in \mathcal{E}^\star$ do
        if (Mapping1-N(S, $S_j^\star$)) then
            $\mathcal{Q}^\diamond \leftarrow$ CombinePaths($E_{i,j}^\star$);
            for each candidate query $Q^\diamond \in \mathcal{Q}^\diamond$ do
                if (VerifyJoinCondition($Q^\diamond$)) then
                    $Q^\star \leftarrow$ ConstructQuery($Q^\diamond$);
                    $\mathcal{Q}^{rec} \leftarrow$ QueryReformulation($Q^\star$, $S_j^\star$, XMAP($S_j^\star$));
                    if ($|\mathcal{Q}^{rec}| > 0$) then
                        $\mathcal{Q}^\star \leftarrow \mathcal{Q}^\star \cup \mathcal{Q}^{rec}$;
                    $\mathcal{Q}^\star \leftarrow \mathcal{Q}^\star \cup Q^\star$;
        else
            if (VerifyJoinCondition($E_{i,j}^\star$)) then
                $Q^\star \leftarrow$ ConstructQuery($Q^\diamond$);
                $\mathcal{Q}^{rec} \leftarrow$ QueryReformulation($Q^\star$, $S_j^\star$, XMAP($S_j^\star$));
                if ($|\mathcal{Q}^{rec}| > 0$) then
                  $\mathcal{Q}^\star \leftarrow \mathcal{Q}^\star \cup \mathcal{Q}^{rec}$;
                $\mathcal{Q}^\star \leftarrow \mathcal{Q}^\star \cup Q^\star$;
    return $\mathcal{Q}^\star$
end

Fig. 3. Pseudo-code of the XMAP reformulation algorithm

4   The Grid Data Integration System (GDIS)

In this section, we describe the deployment and usage of the XMAP reformulation algorithm in the *Grid Data Integration System* (GDIS). GDIS is a decentralized service-based data integration architecture for Grid databases; it has been presented in a previous work [15]. The main purpose of this system is the reconciliation of data sources heterogeneity.

In order to gather the challenges required to address data heterogeneity among Grid-enabled databases, the GDIS architecture is characterized by the features sketched below. GDIS adopts a decentralized approach that can effectively exploit the available Grid resources and their dynamic allocation. Moreover, schema mapping in GDIS is conveniently done to take advantage of Grid flexibility and dynamic nature, so allowing a wide-scale, ad hoc-nature data sharing. Finally, as the Grid aims at realizing the sharing and cooperation of resources among virtual organizations, when queries are posed using a node schema, answers should come from anywhere in the system. GDIS supports these issues by adopting the XMAP integration formalism and also implementing the XMAP query reformulation algorithm described in the previous section.

The GDIS system offers a wrapper/mediator-based approach to integrate data sources: it adopts the XMAP decentralized mediator approach to handle semantic heterogeneity over data sources, whereas syntactic heterogeneity is hidden behind ad-hoc wrappers. In the GDIS architecture (see [15] and Figure 4), the query reformulation engine is run by the *data integration nodes*. Specifically, these nodes offer: (i) a set of data integration utilities allowing to establish mappings, and (ii) the query reformulation algorithm introduced by the XMAP integration formalism. These utilities are exposed through the "portTypes" of the proposed OGSA-GDI data integration service.

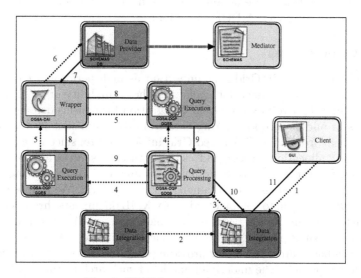

Fig. 4. GDIS functional architecture

GDIS is designed as a service-based distributed architecture where each node exposes all its resources as Grid services except data resources and data integration facility that are exposed as Grid Data Services (GDSs) [16]. In so doing, the GDIS system introduces the OGSA-based *Grid Data Integration* (GDI) service that extends OGSA-DAI and OGSA-DQP portTypes with additional functionality both to enable users to specify semantic mappings (in the form of XMAP documents) among a set of data sources, and to execute the XMAP query rewriting algorithm. Among the portTypes introduced by GDI, two are pertinent to XMAP:

- the *Manual Mappings Composition* portType, through which a client manually builds schema mappings stored in the form of an XMAP document as Service Data Elements (SDE);
- the *Query Reformulation Algorithm* (QRA) portType, that performs the XMAP query reformulation algorithm and receives as input a query and the schema mappings and produces as output a set of reformulated queries. The reformulated queries will be forwarded to the *Grid Data Service* portType offered by the OGSA-DQP distributed query service (GDQS).

Typical interactions in the system are those that take place when the two following activities are performed: (i) adding new resources to the system, (ii) submitting a query with consequent execution. Naturally, XMAP mostly comes to play in the latter case. More precisely, when the client formulates a query, it sends it to a reformulation engine through the QRA portType of the GDI service (Interaction (1) in Figure 4). The QRA portType implements the reformulation operation that executes the XMAP reformulation algorithm receiving as input the query, in the form of an XML document, and importing the mappings established in the system via the importMappings operation provided by the *Import Mappings* portType of the GDI service (Interaction (2)). Reformulated queries are then transmitted, in the form of an XML document, to the GDQS service via the perform operation of the GDS portType (Interaction (3)). The next interactions (4-9) are the same as those of a typical OGSA-DQP execution.

5   Conclusions

Data management in Grid is as important as high performance computing. Data Integration is a key issue for exploiting the availability of large, heterogeneous, distributed data volumes in Grids. Integration formalisms demand significant advances in middleware for sharing data from diverse distributed sources. So, they can benefit from an OGSA-based Grid infrastructure, since it facilitates dynamic discovery, allocation, access, and use of both data sources and computational resources. For these reasons we designed a framework for integrating heterogeneous XML data sources distributed among nodes of a Grid. We propose a query reformulation algorithm to combine and query XML documents through a decentralized point-to-point mediation based on schema mappings. Moreover, this XML integration formalism is exposed as a Grid Service within the GDIS architecture. GDIS is a service-based architecture for providing data integration in Grids using a decentralized approach. The underlying model of such architecture is discussed and we showed how it fits the XMAP formalism/algorithm. Software prototypes of both the XMAP algorithm and the GDIS system are currently being developed, using the Globus Toolkit 3, and OGSA-DAI and OGSA-DQP services.

Acknowledgements

This work has been partially supported by the FP6 Network of Excellence Core-GRID (Contract IST-2002-004265).

References

1. Antonioletti, M., et al.: OGSA-DAI: Two years on. In: Global Grid Forum 10 — Data Area Workshop. (2004)
2. Alpdemir, M.N., Mukherjee, A., Gounaris, A., Paton, N.W., Watson, P., Fernandes, A.A.A., Fitzgerald, D.J.: OGSA-DQP: A service for distributed querying on the grid. In: EDBT. (2004) 858–861
3. Calvanese, D., Giacomo, G.D., Lenzerini, M., Rosati, R., Vetere, G.: Hyper: A framework for peer-to-peer data integration on grids. In: ICSNW. (2004) 144–157
4. Brezany, P., Woehrer, A., Tjoa, A.M.: Novel mediator architectures for grid information systems. FGCS - Grid Computing: Theory, Methods and Applications. **21** (2005) 107–114
5. Foster, I., Kesselman, C., Nick, J.M., Tuecke, S.: The physiology of the grid: An open grid services architecture for distributed systems integration. Open Grid Service Infrastructure WG, Global Grid Forum (2002) `http://www.globus.org/research/ .papers/ogsa.pdf`.
6. Sandholm, T., Gawor, J.: Globus toolkit 3 core — A grid service container framework. Globus Toolkit Core White Paper (2003) `http://www-unix.globus.org/toolkit/ 3.0/ogsa/docs/gt3_core.pdf`.
7. Sheth, A.P., Larson, J.A.: Federated database systems for managing distributed, heterogeneous, and autonomous databases. ACM Computing Surveys **22** (1990) 183–236
8. Lenzerini, M.: Data integration: A theoretical perspective. In: PODS. (2002) 233–246
9. Levy, A.Y., Rajaraman, A., Ordille, J.J.: Querying heterogeneous information sources using source descriptions. In: VLDB. (1996) 251–262
10. Bernstein, P.A., Giunchiglia, F., Kementsietsidis, A., Mylopoulos, J., Serafini, L., Zaihrayeu, I.: Data management for peer-to-peer computing : A vision. In: WebDB. (2002) 89–94
11. Calvanese, D., Damaggio, E., Giacomo, G.D., Lenzerini, M., Rosati, R.: Semantic data integration in P2P systems. In: DBISP2P. (2003) 77–90
12. Franconi, E., Kuper, G.M., Lopatenko, A., Serafini, L.: A robust logical and computational characterisation of peer-to-peer database systems. In: DBISP2P. (2003) 64–76
13. Halevy, A.Y., Suciu, D., Tatarinov, I., Ives, Z.G.: Schema mediation in peer data management systems. In: ICDE. (2003) 505–516
14. Clark, J., DeRose, S.: XML path language (XPath) version 1.0. W3C Recommendation (1999) `http://www.w3.org/TR/xpath`.
15. Comito, C., Talia, D.: GDIS: A service-based architecture for data integration on grids. In: GADA. (2004) 88–98
16. Foster, I., Tuecke, S., Unger, J.: OGSA data services. DAIS-WG Informational Draft, 9th Global Grid Forum (2003)

Towards Dynamic Information Integration

Jürgen Göres

University of Kaiserslautern, Heterogeneous Information Systems Group
`goeres@informatik.uni-kl.de`

Abstract. To utilize the full potential of structured or semi-structured data stored across different information systems, users and applications must not be confronted directly with the individual, heterogeneous data sources, but instead be supplied with a customized integrated view on the data. Traditional information integration is relying on a human-driven process to accomplish this task. While feasible in static, closed-world scenarios, this approach fails in settings like the nascent data grids, which are characterized by a large, permanently changing set of autonomous data sources. We describe the end-to-end integration approach underlying our PALADIN project which aims to reduce and ultimately eliminate the dependency on human experts in the integration process in order to provide fast and cost-effective integration services for these dynamic environments.

1 Introduction

Grid technology aims to provide distributed, potentially global access to computing resources by providing a layer of middleware that abstracts not only from location but ultimately also from the inevitable heterogeneity of these resources. Originating in the area of high performance computing, grids initially focused on the use of CPU and memory resources. In these *computing grids*, the transfer of data is inherently file-based, as it was initially understood only as part of the general infrastructure to pass job executables, input data and results between grid nodes. The good reliability and performance characteristics of this infrastructure led to the adoption of grid technology as a means to provide a large distributed storage space for data-intensive research projects like particle physics. While they are often called *data grids* by their users, we will refer to them as *storage grids*, as their very nature is still just that of a large container for bulk data stored in files, which – from the perspective of the grid – have no discernable structure. Given the massive amounts of raw data these distributed file systems have to deal with, the focus of research and development is on performance and replication aspects.

Today, the understanding of the term data grid is moving away from this file-centric virtual hard disk, towards a grid where preexisting structured or semi-structured data stored in databases is the resource of interest. Thousands of publicly available databases already exist, for example, in areas like life sciences and space observation. However, access to these sources is far from being uniform,

J.-M. Pierson (Ed.): VLDB DMG 2005, LNCS 3836, pp. 16–29, 2005.

based on proprietary interfaces. Beyond these technical barriers, users are faced with different data models, each offering many degrees of design freedom that result in schemas with largely differing structures even when modelling the same real-world concepts. To make things worse, the vocabulary used to describe these concepts is inconsistent even in comparably narrow fields of interest.

Current development in standardization bodies like the Data Access and Integration working group of the GGF focuses on defining interfaces that abstract from technical heterogeneity by building on the well-established web service technology. However, plain access is not sufficient to effectively use data coming from different data sources available on a future data grid, but only represents a necessary first step in the development of data*base* grids. To truly benefit from publicly available data sources, users and applications require a transparent, integrated view on the distributed data sources that abstracts not only from different hardware, operating systems, protocols and interfaces, but also from the logical and semantical heterogeneity among the schemas of these sources.

Providing such an integrated view requires a mapping from the data source schemas to the integrated schema that adapts the different data models and structures as well as the diverging uses and understandings of terms in these schemas. In conventional integration scenarios, which deal with fixed requirements and a relatively stable set of data sources under a single administrative control, this mapping is developed in a human-driven process, involving experts both of information integration and of the respective application domain. We argue that while existing approaches to information integration are appropriate under these static circumstances, they are unsuitable for the ad hoc nature of cooperation and the high degree of autonomy of the data sources in a grid environment, due to their heavy reliance on human expertise and the resulting cost and delay.

In this paper, we describe an end-to-end process to automate information integration that is customized to the dynamic nature of data grids. We start with the analysis of the user requirements for the desired integrated database, followed by the discovery of data sources that can contribute. Next, a mapping is created between these sources' schemas and the integrated schema, which is then deployed in a runtime environment.

This process serves as blueprint for our current research project PALADIN (Pattern-based Approach to LArge-scale Dynamic INformation integration). We describe the basic elements of PALADIN's infrastructure as well as two central concepts we use to augment and ultimately replace human expertise in the integration process: *Domain schemas*, essentially data-centric ontologies, provide machine-processable domain knowledge by describing the concepts of a given application domain and their relationships. *Integration patterns* are used to declaratively describe common problem constellations encountered when mapping between heterogeneous schemas and to specify an approach to their solution, which can then be adapted and applied to the concrete problem.

The remainder of this paper is structured as follows: Section 2 discusses related work. Section 3 gives a short overview of the five conceptual phases of information integration and identifies and describes the essential elements of the PALADIN infrastructure. Section 4 elaborates on each phase in more detail and introduces the concept of integration patterns, which provide the necessary knowledge for the creation of integration plans. Section 5 concludes with a summary and an outlook on future work.

2   Related Work

Foster et al. [1] propose the concept of *virtual organizations*, new forms of short-to medium-term cooperations, which are formed by companies or research institutes to pool computing resources in order to pursue a common goal. The authors explicitly mention data itself as a key resource, which makes virtual organizations a prime beneficiary of dynamic information integration.

Building on a stateful extension of the ubiquitous web services technology, the Global Grid Forum (GGF) is currently standardizing interfaces, architecture and protocols to consolidate different grid projects. Building on this basic infrastructure, the Data Access and Integration working group (DAIS) [2] is specifying interfaces that allow access to data and metadata of data sources with different data models. While still under development, these interfaces will provide a starting point for our proposed integration solution by abstracting from the technical heterogeneity of different data sources based on the same data model. In conjunction with the general grid infrastructure standard interfaces allow us to focus on the logical and semantical heterogeneity specific to information integration.

A number of projects deal with the mapping between data models, most notably between the relational and the XML world. For example, [3] presents two algorithms that create an XML schema from a given relational schema, while [4] describes an approach for the inverse direction. While such algorithms excel in certain situations, they do not produce good results under all circumstances. Another major limitation is the lack of a generally accepted mapping language or operator algebra that can handle XML and SQL alike. Therefore, most algorithms only produce a schema definition in the desired target data model, but do not provide an actual mapping specification that translates the data between the source and target schema, e.g., a view definition that uses SQL/XML. Those that do are generally aimed at a specific runtime environment, like one of the various XML extensions provided by RDBMS vendors.

To solve schematic heterogeneity, it is often necessary to transform information that is modelled as data in one schema and as metadata in the other, which goes beyond the capabilities of most existing query languages and algebras. While XQuery provides sufficient expressiveness for the XML data model, even the latest incarnations of the SQL standard have nothing to offer in this department. SchemaSQL [5] is an extension of SQL that uses an augmented FROM clause to operate not only on table rows but also on the tables of a schema or the attributes of a single table. While significantly improving the expressive power of standard SQL, it only facilitates the manual definition of schematic mappings and is not supported by any commercial DBMS.

An essential aspect to resolving semantic heterogeneity is the discovery of correspondencies between schema elements of different data sources. While this *schema matching* is traditionally done manually by application domain experts, different approaches to semi-automatic schema matching have been proposed (see [6]). The most promising approaches like Cupid [7] combine a large number of techniques from various areas like information retrieval or artificial intelligence into so-called hybrid matchers. These matchers, however, are monolithic, which limits their flexibility when it comes to supporting new data models or adding new matching techniques. In addition, although existing matchers yield respectable results, their general quality is insufficient to solely depend on them for automated integration. Current state of the art can only identify matches as a starting point for the user, who then must be provided with an interface (like the Clio matching tool presented in [8]) to review, correct and amend the results of automatic matching.

As presented by Halevy [9], the definition of mappings from the data sources to the integrated schema can be understood as a variant of the problem of answering queries using views. The work presented there is however limited to the Datalog data model, while our approach can support arbitrary data models.

McBrien and Poulovassilis [10] also use a graph-oriented data model to represent schemas of arbitrary data models. However, they use a fixed set of atomic graph transformations, which, given a mapping from a schema A to another schema B, allows them to automatically derive an inverse mapping or repair an existing mapping during schema evolution [11].

3 Conceptual Process and Infrastructure

Information integration can roughly be structured into five distinct phases as shown in figure 1:

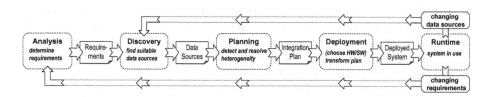

Fig. 1. Phases of Information Integration

Initially, the requirements on the virtual integrated data source are determined, i.e., the desired data model and schema (analysis phase). Based on these results, the set of available data sources is analyzed to discover those that can contribute to the integrated schema (discovery phase). With the target and source schemas as input, the planning phase has to determine a mapping definition that translates the data model, structure and vocabulary of the source schemas into those defined by the target schema. This mapping or *integration plan*, which is still independent of a particular runtime platform, is then deployed to a runtime environment (deployment phase), after which the integrated system is ready for use (runtime phase). Joining or leaving data sources will trigger a (possibly partial) repetition of the process starting with the discovery phase, while changing user or application requirements will trigger a restart beginning with the analysis.

While each phase has individual characteristics, certain concepts and a basic infrastructure are relevant throughout the entire process: A *unified metamodel*, which extends the concepts and terminology of CWM [12], facilitates the handling of arbitrary data models. A flexible *schema matching framework* is used to resolve semantic discrepancies between different schemas, augmented by external application domain knowledge provided in a machine-processable way as *domain schemas*.

3.1   Unified Metamodel

The individual data sources on a data grid use one of a large number of possible data models, each having its own concepts, modelling techniques and notations. Even within a data model, representations are far from being uniform due to different vendor implementations or meta languages. While SQL and XML are the dominating technologies of the day, a large share of the worlds data is still stored in legacy systems with proprietary data models. Information integration in the grid can therefore not limit itself to a fixed set of supported data models, but rather needs a method to uniformly handle arbitrary schemas and any new data model. An existing approach for extensible, integrated metadata handling is OMG's *Common Warehouse Metamodel* [12]. Being a reference metamodel and no actual implementation, it specifies a stack of four distinct meta layers M_0 to M_3. Models on a layer M_i are described by instantiating the elements of the layer M_{i+1} above and can themselves be instantiated to create objects on the layer M_{i-1} below. On the topmost layer M_3 the *Meta Object Facility* (MOF) serves as a meta-metamodel to specify arbitrary metamodels. Using the MOF, the CWM specification provides predefined metamodels (M_2) for SQL, XML, the UML object model and many others. On the M_1 layer, these metamodels are instantiated to create actual schemas or models. The data stored in these schemas finally resides on the M_0 or data layer.

While the CWM's principal concept is sound, it has several drawbacks that impede its use for data and metadata in PALADIN. Besides it overwhelming complexity, which makes implementation and use difficult, the current specification is outdated. For example, the XML metamodel is based on the rather limited expressiveness of DTDs. While this can be easily remedied by using the MOF, the most severe limitation is the lack of a proper data layer. Designed for the handling of metadata only, the CWM provides only a makeshift instance metamodel for sample data. Being a metamodel, it not only violates CWM's own concept of a stack of meta layers, but inevitably results in an unnatural and cumbersome data representation. As a proper M_0 layer representation is a central aspect of the integration patterns described in section 4.2, this major drawback in itself advocates the redesign of a unified metamodel.

The current prototype PALADIN metamodel (PMM) is a simplified Java-based implementation of the CWM that uses code generation to simulate the multiple levels of instantiation. Like CWM, we use an abstract core metamodel whose classes are extended by concrete metamodel classes in order to capture common properties. We provide definitions and import filters for the core parts of the standard SQL:1999 metamodel as well as for XML. Two other metamodels, Match and Domain Schema are briefly discussed in the following sections.

3.2   Schema Matching

While existing schema matching techniques show promising results, the individual matchers only cover a small subset of possible approaches to find correspondencies between or possibly within schemas. Existing hybrid matchers are monolithic, i.e., they provide a number of matching concepts and ideas hardwired into a single algorithm, which makes extension with new and reuse of existing concepts difficult. We are therefore developing an extensible schema matching framework that captures individual approaches as components, which can then be wired together in an arbitrary fashion. Preprocessing components like stemming mechanisms or dictionary and thesaurus lookup operate on the labels of the schema elements. Structural matchers, for example, a variant of the Cupid algorithm, can aggregate correspondencies between individual elements. To combine the results of different matching approaches into a final result, we currently explore different composite matchers. With the flexibility given by this framework, we can improve over the quality of existing individual matchers. To store the results of the matching process, we have defined a Match metamodel. Besides generic matches that indicate 1:1, 1:n and n:m correspondencies between schema elements, we provide matches with more specific semantics, e.g., a sub- or superclass relationship, partial or incomplete union.

3.3   Domain Schemas

Domain knowledge is a key factor in providing a correct mapping from a given set of data sources into a consistent integrated data source that meets user requirements. Schema matching can help to identify correspondencies between schemas, but is not able to provide external knowledge about the application domain that is missing from the schemas. To substitute the human experts in classical integration scenarios, we use *domain schemas* to capture a domain's terms and concepts and their relationships in a machine-understandable way, to serve as a reference during information integration. In PMM, domain schemas are represented in a dedicated object-oriented metamodel. A domain schema's backbone is the directed acyclic graph (DAG) formed by the (multiple-)inheritance hierarchy between its classes, providing a natural broader/narrower-term relationship which can be used both as a thesaurus and as a means to address subdomains with path expressions. By allowing each concept to have several labels in multiple languages, domain schemas can also serve as a dictionary and for synonym lookup. Additional relationships and attributes can be used to add further information, like hints to potential references (e.g., foreign keys that were not explicitly defined in a schema) and strong or weak candidate keys.

4   Integration Phases

Building on the PALADIN infrastructure, the following sections describe how each of the five conceptual phases of information integration has to be implemented in order to be applicable to the dynamic nature of the grid environment. We focus on the pivotal integration planning phase, where we elaborate on the concept of integration patterns.

4.1   Analysis and Discovery

In a traditional integrated system, the user is provided with a fixed, predefined integrated schema in a given data model. In the light of a large number of grid users with individual and changing requirements, a query system on a data grid has to discard this rigid assumption. Instead the user or application developer specifies a schema in a common data definition language, thereby establishing the desired target data model. While this *explicit target schema definition* is suitable if a precise target schema has already been designed, the dynamic nature of the grid makes an *ad-hoc-querying* functionality desirable to explore the available data: The user writes a query using a data modelling language of the favored target data model, and by using terms for table, element or attribute names, etc., he implicitly defines the query's underlying schema. A few minor restrictions, like enforcing the use of correlation names in an SQL query, allow the inference of a basic target schema. While certainly useful for surveying available data, this ad hoc mode will generally not deliver consistent results for a sequence of queries, as each of them usually only touches a few topics of the application domain. Therefore, the implicit schemas of the different queries will likely yield different data sources during discovery. As an alternative to schema inference on the basis of individual queries, we propose a *schema-by-example* approach: The user issues several queries, which are then aggregated into a single target schema. The target schema is represented in the PMM.

In addition to determining the target schema, the desired quality of service (QoS) can be specified either implicitly, by assuming reasonable defaults depending on the method used to obtain the target schema, or explicitly with a QoS definition language. QoS can include aspects like a source's trustworthiness, costs or availability.

With the target schema defined in the vocabulary of the user or programmer, sources that can contribute data and meet the QoS requirements have to be discovered. To determine usable data sources, each source's schema can be retrieved, matched with the target schema and those that do not show any correspondencies can be discarded. While this is practicable in small-world scenarios with a limited number of fixed data sources, it is infeasible in a global data grid with an ever growing set of data sources.

To reduce the set of data sources that have to be analyzed in detail, sources are cataloged in grid resource directories on the basis of application domains, by using the unique identifiers of the respective domain schemas that fully or partially overlap the sources' schemas. As domains can be large, path expressions on the class hierarchy (or the directed acyclic graph resulting from multiple inheritance) of a domain schema can be used to further narrow down a source's topics. Still the remaining candidate sources can be numerous.

To further speed up the selection, *indirect schema matching* can be performed as shown in figure 2: Initially (a), each source schema and the target schema are matched against the relevant domain schema(s).

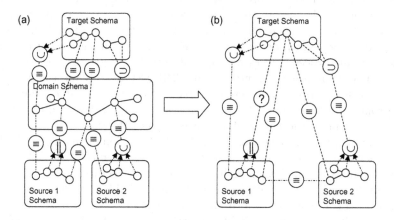

Fig. 2. Indirect Schema Matching

By using the domain schemas as a reference and assuming transitivity for matches, direct matches between the schemas can now be inferred (b). The number of match processes for n schemas and d relevant domains is effectively reduced from $O(n^2)$ required for the pairwise matching of all schemas to $O(n \cdot d)$, as each (source or target) schema now has to be matched against the relevant domain schemas only. The number of relevant domains d depends on the scope of the target schema and is usually comparably small, so this reduction already represents a significant improvement. However, the greatest gain results from the fact that domain schemas can be considered relatively stable. Therefore, correspondencies between the data source schemas and those domain schemas relevant to the individual source do not have to be determined during the discovery process, but can instead be identified in advance by the data source provider. This allows to invest more time and effort to discover these matches, making the use of more elaborate manual or semi-automatical schema matching approaches possible. So effectively all that remains to be done during the discovery phase is for the user or the system to choose a set of domain schemas that are relevant for the target schema and match these with it, further reducing the number of schema matches to $O(d)$.

As the results of this *indirect schema matching* can produce overly optimistic correspondencies between the schemas, the best-matching sources can optionally be matched directly with the target schema to remove uncertainties introduced by the indirection, using the indirect matches as starting point.

4.2 Integration Planning

With the set of candidate sources and the target schema, the integration planning phase can commence, i.e., the definition of a mapping that transforms the data found in the source schemas into the terms and structure of the target schema. This phase is particularly reliant on humans. With their application expertise they can understand the precise semantics hidden in the structure of the different schemas and then use their experience to define the appropriate mappings. In order to reduce this reliance, a method is needed to capture human expertise and experience and provide it to an integration planning system in a reusable and machine-processable way. One could apply the idea of case-based reasoning (CBR) to information integration. CBR systems rely on a large number of cases, each describing a concrete problem with its associated solution. When confronted with a new problem, these systems try to find the case that most closely resembles the new problem scenario and then try to adapt its solution to this new problem. However, both the identification of the most suitable case and its customization can be difficult, especially when cases describe situations that are more complex than plain attribute-value vectors.

Our concept of integration patterns follows a different approach: A pattern describes a common problem situation in a generic way and provides a guideline to resolve it, which can be adapted to each specific situation. A straightforward representation of a pattern is an algorithm that searches the set of schemas for the problem situation the pattern can solve. Once this situation is identified, the algorithm can then apply the solution, i.e., modify the affected parts of the schema(s) and create a description of how to transform the data found in the original schema structure. However, such an imperative description of patterns makes their development, maintenance and extension difficult and also makes them dependent on a specific implementation of the uniform metamodel. So, in order to allow an easy extension of the library of available patterns without programming effort, a declarative notation has to be provided.

Such a language has to offer sufficient expressiveness to describe all kinds of structural, schematic and data model transformations. While a number of existing languages come into consideration, each has its limitations: SQL views can transform relational schemas and data and in conjunction with extensions like SQL/XML they can also transform relational data to XML. However, the inverse transformation is not possible, and SQL is unable to bridge the gap between data and metadata (i.e. resolve schematic heterogeneity). Approaches like SchemaSQL remedy this situation, but are still limited to the relational data model. XQuery offers sufficient expressiveness to turn data to metadata and vice versa, but is limited to the XML realm alone. So we might be tempted to define yet another bloated SQL-like language, with the severe drawback that every new metamodel we add will also likely require new language constructs.

A natural alternative is viewing both metadata and data described with the PALADIN metamodel as a typed, attributed multigraph. That way, we can describe patterns as transformations of the PMM graphs. Graph transformation is a well-explored concept (see [13]). To represent integration patterns, we chose an approach that is based on the semi-graphical language defined for the PROGRES graph replacement system [14]. While the graphical elements provide an easily readable, yet semantically precise description of the most relevant aspects of a pattern, the textual notation adds expressiveness that would be hard to capture graphically. A graph transformation is described using production rules. A production rule has a left-hand side (LHS) that describes the situation it can be applied to as an abstract subgraph, and a right-hand side (RHS) that describes the result of the rule's application. To connect left- and right-hand side, every element that should be preserved by the pattern is bound to a variable. An element that is not repeated on the RHS indicates a deletion, an element that is new on the RHS indicates the creation of an element.

Every integration pattern is represented by two interdependent production rules (*facets*). Figure 3 shows the (simplified) pattern `denormalize` that describes the necessary operations on two tables of two source schemas whose contents need to be joined into a single table of the target schema. More patterns and examples of their use are presented in [15].

The first facet `denormalize().m1` operates on the M_1 or model layer. Its LHS describes the constellation that has to be encountered in the schema graph in order for the pattern to be applicable. The LHS also assigns identifiers to relevant schema elements, which the RHS and the M_0 facet can refer to later. To use the `denormalize` pattern, there have to be two source schemas (labeled *s1* and *s2*) that each have a table *t1* and *t2*. Both tables must have a set of columns (*t1rc* and *t2rc*) which represent a reference *r* between the tables. This reference might have been identified during schema matching. Each table can optionally (indicated by the dotted lines) have further columns (*t1oc*, *t2oc*) which are not involved in the reference. If such a situation is encountered, the pattern can be applied, with the results described using the RHS of the M_1 facet: A new table *t3* is attached to schema *s1* and takes ownership of all columns of the tables *t1* and *t2*, except the *t2rc* columns, which – being redundant after the join operation – are deleted, as are the two original tables. The schema *s2*, however, is repeated on the RHS and is thus preserved, as it might still contain other tables or views. All edges to a node in a pattern that are not explicitly mentioned on its LHS (*context edges*) are preserved if the node itself is preserved, otherwise they are deleted. Alternatively, the diamond symbol can be used to redirect context edges of deleted nodes. This is used in the example to indicate that all edges to the deleted *t1*, *t2* and *t2rc* nodes are redirected to *t3* and *t1rc* respectively.

To define the effects on the data stored in the schema elements, the second facet on the M_0 layer references the instances of the schema elements in the M_1 facet using the identifiers defined there. In the example, the LHS describes

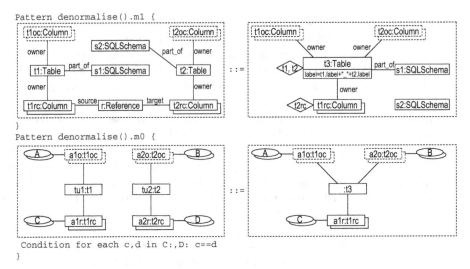

Fig. 3. An integration pattern expressed as a graph transformation

the tuples *tu1* and *tu2* of the tables *t1* and *t2* with their respective attributes (*a1o*, *a1r*, *a2o*, *a2r*) and the literal values of these attributes (*A* to *D*). The RHS uses these elements to construct a result tuple of the newly created table *t3*, by attaching the attributes *a1o*, *a2o* and *a1r* with their respective literals to the new *t3* tuple. The textual notation is used to express an equi-join, i.e., only those pairs of tuples *tu1* and *tu2* of the LHS are transformed into a *t3* tuple, whose values for the *a1r* and *a2r* attributes are pairwise equal.

While this simplified example pattern does not go beyond the capabilities of a relational view definition, the expressiveness of graph transformation allows the definition of arbitrary operators that have no equivalent in existing query languages or operator algebras, like the transformation of metadata to data and vice versa, or transformation between different data models [15].

To find out which patterns are appropriate for an integration problem, i.e., a set of source schemas and a target schema, a graph replacement system tries to find matches of the LHSs of the patterns' M_1 facets. If the problem is found in the graph representing the source schemas, the suggested solution of the RHS is compared to the target schema. If the similarity to the target schema is higher than before, the pattern becomes a possible candidate. If more than one pattern matches in a given situation, the increase in similarity can be used for a simple greedy heuristic to choose the pattern that is applied first. The process is repeated on the resulting intermediate schema graph, until either the target schema or a dead-end is reached. In the latter case, backtracking is performed. To reduce the complexity of pattern search, an index based on the type of nodes can be used to limit the search to promising regions of a schema graph. More advanced heuristics can also reduce the overhead of matching all patterns against the entire schema graph: By structuring the planning process into distinct phases, first transforming all schemas into the desired data model, then performing schematic adaptation and finally unifying their structure, the number of simultaneously active patterns can be reduced.

Given a sufficiently large library of patterns, the task of integration planning can now be understood as proving a hypothesis (the target schema) from a set of axioms (the source schemas) using a set of rules (the patterns). Any successful deduction, i.e., a sequence of pattern applications, describes an abstract query graph or *integration plan* that transforms the source data into the desired target schema, with each pattern's M_0 facet representing an operator in this graph.

In order to facilitate the definition of patterns for cases where the added expressiveness of graph transformations is not needed, e.g. when transforming data within a single data model, a high-level language (e.g. SQL, SchemaSQL, XQuery) can be used to specify the pattern's effects. This representation is then compiled into an equivalent graph transformation.

4.3   Deployment and Runtime

To use an abstract integration plan discovered in the previous phase, it has to be deployed to a runtime environment (RE). However, neither will existing REs be able to directly implement the graph-oriented integration plan, nor is it desirable to handle large amounts of data as graph transformations, especially if an equivalent native operator exists. Instead we should reuse existing integration systems wherever possible. This requires the translation of the abstract plan into a logical plan using the languages and facilities provided by the chosen runtime environment (RE). To this end, deployment rules for each supported RE define how the abstract operators of the integration plan are mapped to the available RE operations. For example, if the data sources are relational or supported by relational wrappers, an existing integration system like IBM's Information Integrator [16] can provide sufficient functionality, and the abstract plans are translated to a number of view definitions and wrapper configurations.

The integration tool is made available as a factory service that provides an interface to deploy such plans and create a new service instance, e.g., a Grid Data Service that provides access to the new virtual integrated database. The plan can also be used for replication-oriented integration with an ETL tool, with the resulting replicated data warehouse being put on the grid. A more grid-like RE will abandon these heavy-weight services and instead implement individual operators as grid services. The plan created by the integration planning service will be used to find the required operators via common directory services. Depending on the performance of individual nodes, available network bandwidth, etc., an integration plan can be widely distributed, the individual operator services being choreographed using a language like BPEL or the data-flow-oriented *perform* documents specified by OGSA-DAI. If a given logical operator is not supported natively by the RE, a generic graph-based operator can serve as fallback if the RE provides an appropriate extension mechanism. This generic operator can be configured with the graph representation of the missing operator.

After the chosen RE has been set up, the user can access it, e.g., via a Grid Data Service interface. Depending on the QoS requirements and the estimated usage time, changes in the available data sources may invalidate the integration plan. If stability of the data in the integrated schema is not absolutely necessary, discovery, planning and deployment can be triggered automatically and transparently. If up-to-dateness of the data is most relevant, a deployed plan can be verified from time to time to discover and integrate any new data sources.

5   Conclusion and Future Work

We presented our concept for information integration in the dynamic environment of data grids. In order to reduce and ultimately remove the need for human experts to set up an integration solution, we sketched our basic concepts to capture experience in a reusable, machine-processable way: Domain schemas in conjunction with advanced schema matching methods provide knowledge of the application domain and help resolve semantic heterogeneity. Integration patterns are used to convey experience in solving structural and schematic conflicts between source and target schemas.

Emphasis of our current work is on the evaluation of alternative implementations of the PALADIN metamodel and on the suitability of existing graph matching engines for integration planning with patterns. We also analyze if schema matching itself can be done in-band with the pattern mechanism, as schema matching essentially introduces additional nodes and edges into a graph representing previously unconnected schemas.

PALADIN is currently aimed at read-only access as updates considerably raise the demands on the soundness of an integration plan. However, patterns can also address the well-known view update problem, as they can respect the semantics of the specific situation and provide appropriate update rules.

We are also analyzing the decidability properties of our integration planning system: If a pattern application strategy and a schema similarity measure, applied to a set of source and target schemas and a pattern library, do not yield a deduction after a given time, this does not imply that a deduction does not exist, but only that none has been found, which translates to Turing's halting problem. Proper criteria have yet to be defined to decide when to discard a deduction path and start backtracking or when to give up integration planning entirely. These decisions are currently made based on heuristics and timeouts.

Although our current focus is on the integration planning phase, the deployment of abstract integration plans to a concrete runtime environment is in itself a challenging topic. The deployment rules for different runtime environments can themselves be considered machine-processable knowledge, i.e., patterns. However, this kind of patterns does not possess the closure property of our integration planning patterns, as the results of their use (i.e., the concrete integration plans) are outside our metamodel. Concepts for the uniform handling of all kinds of possible plan representations are subject of future work.

References

1. Foster, I., Kesselman, C., Tuecke, S.: The Anatomy of the Grid – Enabling Scalable Virtual Organizations. In: Proceedings of the First IEEE International Symposium on Cluster Computing and the Grid (CCGrid 2001), IEEE Computer Society (May 15–18, 2001)
2. Antonioletti, M., Atkinson, M., Malaika, S., Laws, S., Paton, N.W., Pearson, D., Riccardi, G.: The Grid Data Service Specification (September 19th, 2003)
3. Lee, D., Mani, M., Chiu, F., Chu, W.W.: NeT and CoT: Translating Relational Schemas to XML Schemas using Semantic Constraints. In: Proceedings of the 2002 ACM CIKM International Conference on Information and Knowledge Management. (November 4–9 2002)
4. Lee, D., Chu, W.W.: CPI: Constraints-Preserving Inlining Algorithm for Mapping XML DTD to Relational Schema. Data and Knowledge Engineering **39** (October 2001) 3–25
5. Lakshmanan, L.V.S., Sadri, F., Subramanian, I.N.: SchemaSQL – A Language for Interoperability in Relational Multi-Database Systems. In: Proceedings of the 22nd VLDB Conference. (1996) 239–250
6. Rahm, E., Bernstein, P.A.: A survey of approaches to automatic schema matching. VLDB Journal **10** (2001) 334–350
7. Madhavan, J., Bernstein, P.A., Rahm, E.: Generic Schema Matching with Cupid. In: Proceedings of the 27th VLDB Conference. (2001) 49–58
8. Popa, L., Velegrakis, Y., Miller, R.J., Hernández, M.A., Fagin, R.: Translating Web Data. In: Proceedings of the 28th VLDB Conference. (2002) 598–609
9. Halevy, A.Y.: Answering queries using views: A survey. VLDB Journal **10** (2001) 270–294
10. McBrien, P., Poulovassilis, A.: A Uniform Approach to Inter-model Transformations. 11th International Conference on Advanced Information Systems Engineering CAiSE'99 (June 14–18, 1999) 333–348
11. McBrien, P., Poulovassilis, A.: Schema evolution in heterogeneous database architectures, a schema transformation approach. 14th International Conference on Advanced Information Systems Engineering CAiSE 2002 (May 27–31, 2002) 484–499
12. Object Management Group: Common Warehouse Metamodel (CWM) Specification Version 1.1. (March 2003)
13. Schürr, A.: Programmed Graph Replacement Systems. In: Handbook of Graph Grammars and Computing by Graph Transformations. (1997) 479–546
14. Schürr, A., Winter, A.W., Zündorf, A.: The PROGRES Approach: Language and Environment. In: Handbook of Graph Grammars and Computing by Graph Transformation. (1997) 487–550
15. Göres, J.: Pattern-based Information Integration in Dynamic Environments. In: Proceedings of the 9th International Database Engineering & Applications Symposium (IDEAS 2005). (July 25–27, 2005) 125–134
16. Bruni, P., Arnaudies, F., Bennett, A., Englert, S., Keplinger, G.: Data Federation with IBM DB2 Information Integrator V8.1. (October 16, 2003)

Adapting to Changing Resource Performance in Grid Query Processing

Anastasios Gounaris[1], Jim Smith[2], Norman W. Paton[1], Rizos Sakellariou[1], Alvaro A.A. Fernandes[1], and Paul Watson[2]

[1] University of Manchester
{gounaris, norm, rizos, alvaro}@cs.man.ac.uk
[2] University of Newcastle upon Tyne
{jim.smith, paul.watson}@ncl.ac.uk

Abstract. The Grid provides facilities that support the coordinated use of diverse resources, and consequently, provides new opportunities for wide-area query processing. However, Grid resources, as well as being heterogeneous, may also exhibit unpredictable, volatile behaviour. Thus, query processing on the Grid needs to be adaptive, in order to cope with evolving resource characteristics, such as machine load. To address this challenge, an architecture is proposed that has been empirically evaluated over a prototype Grid-enabled adaptive query processor instantiating it.

1 Introduction

Grid query processing is particularly relevant where there is a need to integrate information and analysis from different sources for specific periods of time, and to *e-Science* applications, the owners of which, contrary to the typical *e-business* scenario, lack the computational capacity to run some of their tasks and conduct *in-silico* experiments. Especially for the latter case, Grid query processing, like many Grid computations, is likely to place a significant emphasis on high-performance and scalability. Traditionally, query processors often attain scalability and improved performance by relying on the benefits of parallelism. *Pipelined* parallelism has been examined and adopted to different extents in wide-area query processing [15]. Complementarily, query processing can benefit significantly from partitioning the operators within a query execution plan across multiple nodes, a form of parallelism commonly referred to as *intra-operator* or *partitioned* [13], in which all the clones of an operator evaluate a different portion of the same dataset in parallel. GridDB [16] and OGSA-DQP [1] are examples of Grid-enabled database systems that support access to Grid computations and databases, and exploit parallel heterogeneous infrastructures to meet demanding application requirements.

A basic difficulty in efficiently executing a query on the Grid is that the unavailability of accurate statistics at compile time and evolving runtime conditions (such as CPU loads and network bandwidth) may cause load imbalance that detrimentally affects the performance of static techniques for partitioned

J.-M. Pierson (Ed.): VLDB DMG 2005, LNCS 3836, pp. 30–44, 2005.

parallelism. Hence, a challenge for the query processor is to define intra-operator data-partitioning that takes into account these changes. Failing to do so in an efficient way may annul the benefits of parallelism. Just as in homogeneous, controlled environments (e.g., clusters of similar nodes), a slowdown in even a single machine that is not followed by the correct rebalancing, causes the whole system to underperform at the level of the slow machine [2]. To tackle this, the system needs not only to be able to capture these changes as they occur in a wide-area environment, but also to respond to them in a comprehensive, timely and inexpensive manner by devising and deploying appropriate repartitioning policies.

Adaptive load balancing becomes more complicated if the parallelised operations store intermediate state or have incoming queues, like the *hash join* and *exchange* query operators (we call such operators stateful). Assume, for example, that a query optimizer constructs a plan in which there is a hash join parallelised across multiple sites. A hash function applied to the join attribute defines the site for each tuple. In this case, any data repartitioning of unprocessed tuples needs to be accompanied by repartitioning of the hash tables that had already been created within the hash joins.

This paper presents a comprehensive, effective and efficient solution to the problem above. It dynamically rebalances intra-operator parallelism across Grid nodes for both stateful and stateless operations and, in particular, it makes the following contributions:

- It proposes an architecture for *adaptive query processing* (AQP) that is characterised by the following features: it is non-centralised, it is service-oriented, and its components communicate with each other asynchronously according to the publish/subscribe model. Thus it can be applied to loosely-coupled, autonomous environments such as the Grid.
- It presents an implementation of the architecture through extensions to the OGSA-DQP[1] distributed query processor for the Grid [1], demonstrating the practicality of the approach. The resulting prototype has been empirically evaluated and the results show that it can yield significant performance improvements, in some cases by an order of magnitude, in representative examples. In addition, the overhead remains reasonably low, which is important when adaptivity is not required.

The remainder of the paper is structured as follows. The extensions to the static OGSA-DQP system in order to transform it into an adaptive one are presented in Section 2. Section 3 demonstrates adaptations to workload imbalance. Related work is in Section 4, and Section 5 concludes the paper.

2   Grid Services for Adaptive Query Processing

OGSA-DQP has been implemented over the Globus Toolkit 3 Grid middleware. It provides two types of Grid Services to perform static query process-

---

[1] OGSA-DQP is publicly available in open-source form from www.ogsadai.org.uk/dqp.

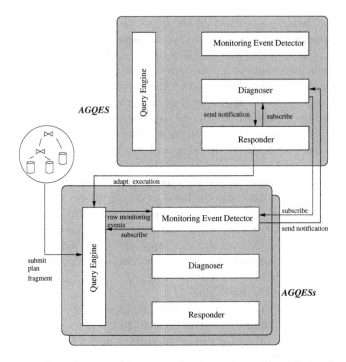

Fig. 1. An adaptive architecture for dynamic workload balancing

ing on the Grid, GDQS (Grid Distributed Query Service) and GQES (Grid Query Evaluation Service). A GDQS contacts resource registries that contain the addresses of the computational and data resources available and updates the metadata catalog of the system. It accepts queries from the users, which are subsequently parsed, optimised, and scheduled employing intra-operator parallelism (e.g., [11]). The query plan consists of a set of subplans that are evaluated by GQESs. A GQES is dynamically created on each machine that has been selected by the GDQS's optimiser to contribute to the execution. GQESs contain the query execution engine, which adopts the *iterator* pipelining model of execution [13]. Data communication is encapsulated within an enhanced *exchange* operator [12], as described later. Inter-service transmission of data blocks is handled by SOAP/HTTP. Remote databases are accessible from the scan operators as GDSs (Grid Data Services) exposed by the generic wrappers developed in the OGSA-DAI project (www.ogsadai.org.uk). Also, arbitrary Web Services can play the role of typed foreign functions and be invoked from queries (with the *operation call* operator being responsible for the execution).

Adaptive GQESs (AGQESs) instantiate a novel architecture for AQP that distinguishes between the *monitoring* (i.e. feedback collection), feedback *assessment*, and *response* stages of adaptations. Each AGQES comprises four components (Fig.1): one for implementing the query operators, thus forming the query engine (which is the only component in static GQESs), and three for adaptivity. The extraction of monitoring information is based on self-monitoring operators, as reported in [10]. As such, the query engine is capable of producing raw, low-level monitoring information (such as the number of tuples each operator has produced so far, and the actual time cost of an operator). The *MonitoringEvent-Detector* component collects such information and acts as a source of notifications on the dynamic behaviour of distributed resources and of query execution. The *Diagnoser* performs the assessment phase, i.e., it establishes whether there is an issue with the current execution (e.g., workload imbalance). The *Responder* decides whether and how to react. Its decisions may affect not only the local query engine, but any query engine participating in the evaluation. The adaptivity components can subscribe to each other and communicate asynchronously via notifications. Note that the above approach implies that the GDQS optimiser need not play any role during adaptations, and the distributed AGQESs encapsulate all the mechanisms required to adjust their execution in a decentralised way.

3   Adapting to Workload Imbalance

3.1   Approach

The execution of a plan fragment over a fixed set of resources is considered to be *balanced* when all the participating machines finish at the same (or about the same) time. Workload imbalance may be the result of uneven load distribution in the case of homogeneous machines, but in the case of heterogeneous machines and the Grid, it might be the result of a distribution that is not proportional to the capabilities of the machines employed (both because the machines are different and because their capabilities are subject to dynamic changes). To achieve workload balance during execution we configure the AGQESs in the following way. The *MonitoringEventDetector* is active in each site evaluating a query fragment, and receives raw monitoring events from the local query engine. There also needs to be one activated *Diagnoser* and one *Responder* that subscribe to the *MonitoringEventDetectors* (Fig.1).

Monitoring. The query engine generates notifications of the following two types:

- **M1**, which contains information about the processing cost of a tuple. Such notifications are generated by the exchange operators that form the local root of subplans (i.e, exchange producers) and include (i) the cost of processing an incoming tuple in milliseconds; (ii) the average waiting time of the subplan leaf operator for this tuple, which corresponds to the idle time that the relevant thread has spent; and (iii) the current selectivity.
- **M2**, which contains information about the communication cost of an outgoing buffer of tuples. Such notifications are generated by exchanges that form the local root of subplans, and include: (i) the cost of sending a buffer in

milliseconds; (ii) the recipient of the buffer; and (iii) the number of tuples that the buffer contains.

These low-level notifications are sent to a *MonitoringEventDetector* component, which:

- groups the notifications of type M1 by the identifier of the operator that generated the notification, and the notifications of the type M2 by the concatenated identifiers of the producer and recipient of the relevant buffer;
- computes the running average of the cost over a window of a certain length, discarding the minimum and maximum values; and
- generates a notification to be sent to subscribed *Diagnoser*, if this average value change by a specified threshold *thresM*.

The default configuration is characterised by the following parameters. The monitoring frequency for the query engine is one notification for each 10 tuples produced (for M1) and one notification for each buffer sent (for M2); the low level notifications from the query engine are sent to the local *MonitoringEventDetector*; the window over which the average is calculated (in the *MonitoringEventDetector*) contains the last 25 events; and the threshold *thresM* to generate notifications for *Diagnosers* is set to 20%. This means that the average processing cost of a tuple needs to change by at least 20%, before the *Diagnoser* is notified. All these values and thresholds are configurable for any component, but determining an optimal setting has left for future work.

Assessment. The assessment is carried out by the *Diagnoser*. The *Diagnoser* gathers information produced by *MonitoringEventDetectors* to establish whether there is workload imbalance. Assume that a subplan p is partitioned across n machines, and that p_i, $i = 1 \ldots n$, is the subplan fragment sent to the ith AGQES. The *MonitoringEventDetectors* notify the cost per processed tuple $c(p_i)$ for each such subplan, as explained earlier. Also the *Diagnoser* is aware of the current tuple distribution policy, which is represented as a vector $W = (w_1, w_2, \ldots, w_n)$, where w_i represents the proportion of tuples that is sent to p_i. To balance execution, the objective is to allocate a workload w_i' to each AGQES that is inversely proportional to $c(p_i)$. The *Diagnoser* computes the balanced vector $W' = (w_1', w_2', \ldots, w_n')$. However, it only notifies the *Responder* with the proposed W' if there exists a pair of w_i and w_i' for which $\frac{|w_i - w_i'|}{w_i}$ exceeds a threshold *thresA*. This is to avoid triggering adaptations with low expected benefit.

The cost per tuple for a subplan $c(p_i)$ can be computed in two ways:

- **A1**, which takes into account only the notifications of type M1 that are produced by the relevant subplan instance; or
- **A2**, which additionally takes into account the notifications of type M2 that are produced by the subplans that deliver data to the relevant subplan instance, and contain the communication costs for this delivery.

The default configuration is characterised by the following parameters. The threshold *thresA* to generate notifications for *Responders* is set to 20%; and the communication cost between subplans in the same machine (i.e., when the exchange producer and consumer reside on the same machine) is considered zero.

Response. For operator state management, the system relies on an infrastructure that has been developed mainly to attain fault tolerance. The description of the fault-tolerance features is out of the scope of this paper; details can be found in [18]. Here, we briefly discuss those features that are used for state repartitioning. Exchanges comprise two parts that can run independently: exchange producers and exchange consumers. The producers insert checkpoint tuples into the set of data tuples they send to their consumers. They also keep a copy of the outgoing data in their local recovery log. When the tuples between two checkpoints have finished processing and are not needed any more by the operators higher up in the query plan, the checkpoints are returned in the form of acknowledgment tuples. In practice, the recovery logs contain, at any point, the tuples that have not finished being processed by the evaluators to which they were sent, and thus include all the in-transit tuples, and the tuples that make up operator states. This provides an opportunity to repartition state across consumer nodes by extracting the tuples stored in the recovery logs, and applying the data repartitioning policy to these tuples as well.

The *Responder* receives notifications about imbalance from the *Diagnoser* in the form of proposed enhanced workload distribution vectors W'. To decide whether to accept this proposal, it contacts all the evaluators that produce data to estimate the progress of execution in line with [7]. If the execution is not close to completion, it notifies the evaluators that need to change their distribution policy, and the *Diagnosers* that need to update the information about the current tuple distribution (i.e, $W \leftarrow W'$). The data distribution can change in two ways:

– **R1**, where the tuples in the recovery logs (i.e., the tuples already buffered to be sent, and the tuples already sent to their consumers but not processed) are redistributed in accordance with the new data distribution policy. We call this redistribution *retrospective*.
– **R2**, where the buffered tuples and the recovery logs are not affected. We call this redistribution *prospective*.

In the R1 case, operator state is effectively recreated in other machines. This may be useful when adaptations need to take effect as soon as possible, and is imperative for redistributing tuples processed by stateful operators (to ensure result correctness).

3.2   Evaluation

The experiments presented in this section show the benefits of redistributing the tuple workload on the fly to keep the evaluation balanced across evaluators, which results in better performance. The main results can be summarised as follows:

– in the presence of perturbed machines, performance (i.e., response time) improves by several factors and the magnitude of degradation, in some cases by an order of magnitude;

- the overhead remains low and no flooding of messages occurs; and
- the system can adapt efficiently even to very rapid changes.

Two example queries are used:

Q1: `select EntropyAnalyser(p.sequence)`
`from protein_sequences p`
Q2: `select i.ORF2 from protein_sequences p,`
`protein_interactions i where i.ORF1=p.ORF;`

The tables *protein_sequences* and *protein_interactions*, along with the *EntropyAnalyser* Web Service operation, are from the OGSA-DQP demo database and they contain data on proteins and results of a bioinformatics experiment, respectively (the *protein_sequences* used in the experiments is slightly modified to make all the tuples the same length to facilitate result analysis). Q1 retrieves and produces 3000 tuples. It is computation-intensive rather than data- or communication-intensive. However, as shown in the experiments, Q1 is chosen in such a way that data communication and retrieval do contribute to the total response time. This contribution is even more significant in Q2, which joins *protein_sequences* with *protein_interactions*, which contains 4700 tuples. So, Q1 and Q2 are complementary to each other: in the former, the most expensive operator is the call to the WS, and in the latter, a traditional operator such as join.

The adaptations described can be applied to an arbitrarily large number of machines. However, as the purpose of the current evaluation is to provide useful insights into the behaviour and effectiveness of the adaptivity policies rather than into how the complete system functions, a carefully controlled experimentation environment is required. Thus two machines are used for the evaluation of *EntropyAnalyser* in Q1, and the join in Q2, unless otherwise stated. The data are retrieved from a third machine. All machines run RedHat Linux 9, are connected by a 100Mbps network, and are autonomously exposed as Grid resources. The third machine retrieves and sends data to the first two as fast as it can. The iterator model is followed, but the incoming queues within exchanges can fit the complete dataset. Due to the pipelined parallelism, the data retrieval is completed independently of the progress of the WS calls and joins. For each result, the query was run three times, and the average is presented here. Finally, we have used two methods to create artificial load leading to machine perturbation: (i) programming a computation to iterate over the same function multiple times, and (ii) inserting *sleep()* calls.

Performance Improvements. This set of experiments demonstrates the capability of AGQESs to degrade their performance gracefully when machines experience perturbations. Thus, they exhibit significantly improved performance compared to static GQESs. In the first experiment, we set the cost of the WS call in Q1 in one machine to be exactly 10 times more than in the other, and the responses are prospective (response type R2). The first row of Table 1 shows how the system behaves under different configurations. More specifically, the columns in the table correspond to the following cases:

Table 1. Performance of queries in normalised units

Query-Response	no ad / no imb	ad / no imb	no ad / imb	ad / imb
Q1 - R2	1	1.059	3.53	1.45
Q1 - R1	1	1.15	3.53	1.57
Q2 - R1	1	1.11	1.71	1.31

- *no ad / no imb:* there is no imbalance between the performance of the two services, and adaptivity is not enabled;
- *ad / no imb:* there is no imbalance between the performance of the two services, and adaptivity is enabled;
- *no ad / imb:* one WS call is ten times costlier than the other, thus there is imbalance between the two services, and adaptivity is not enabled; and
- *ad / imb:* there is imbalance, and adaptivity is enabled.

The results are normalised, so that the response time corresponding to *no ad / no imb* is set to 1 unit for each query. The percentage of degradation due to imbalance is given by the difference of the normalised performance from 1. The "unnecessary" adaptivity overhead is the overhead incurred when adaptivity is not needed (i.e., there is no imbalance)[2], which can be computed by the difference between the second and the third columns of Table 1 (1st row). This difference is 5.9%. When one WS is perturbed and there are no adaptivity mechanisms, the response time of the query increases 3.53 times (4th column in Table 1). For this type of query, the cost to evaluate the WS calls is the highest cost. However, it is not dominant, as there is significant I/O and communication costs. Thus, a 10-fold increase in the WS cost results in a 3.53-fold increase in the query response time. The adaptive system manages to drop this increase to 1.45 times, performing significantly better than without adaptivity (45% increase when adaptivity is enabled as opposed to 253% when it is disabled).

The 2nd row in Table 1 shows the results when the experiment is repeated, and the adaptation is retrospective (type R1 of response). The increase in response time when the adaptivity is not enabled (*no ad / imb*) remains stable as expected (3.53 units). However, the average overhead (*ad / no imb*) is nearly three times more (15.3% of the execution). This is because it is now more costly to perform log management, as the tuples already sent to remote evaluators need to be discarded and redistributed in a tidy manner. Because of the larger overhead, the degradation of the performance in the imbalanced case (*ad / imb*) is larger than for prospective response (1.57 times from 1.45).

The same general pattern is observed for Q2 as well, using the second method to create imbalance artificially. In this case, the perturbation is caused in one

---

[2] Without adaptivity, the machines finish at the same time (the difference is in the order of fractions of seconds). This, in general, cannot be attained in a distributed setting. In more realistic scenarios, adaptivity is very rarely "unnecessary", even when distributed services are expected to behave similarly, but these experiments aim to show the actual overhead.

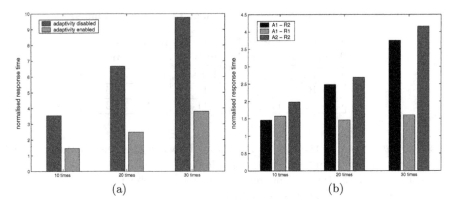

Fig. 2. (a) Performance of Q1 for prospective adaptations; (b) Performance of Q1 for different adaptivity policies

machine by the insertion of a *sleep(10msecs)* call before the processing of each tuple by the join. The 3rd row of Table 1 shows the performance when the adaptations are retrospective. The overhead is 11%, and adaptivity, in the case of imbalance, makes the system run 1.31 times slower instead of 1.71.

Varying the Size of Perturbation. We reran Q1 for the cases in which the perturbed WS is 10, 20 and 30 times costlier, and adaptations are prospective. Fig. 2(a) shows that the improvements in performance are consistent over a reasonably wide range of perturbations. When the WS cost on one of the machines becomes 10, 20 and 30 times costlier, the response time becomes 3.53, 6.66 and 9.76 times higher, respectively, without dynamic balancing. With dynamic balancing, these drop to 1.45, 2.48 and 3.79 times higher, respectively, i.e., the performance improvement is significant consistently.

Effects of Different Policies. Thus far, the assessment has been carried out according to the type A1, in which communication cost is not taken into account. The next experiment takes a closer look at the effects of different adaptivity policies. Three cases are examined: (i) when the *Diagnoser* does not take into account the communication cost to send data to the subplan examined for imbalance, and no state is recreated (type A1 of assessment combined with type R2 of response); (ii) when the *Diagnoser* does not take into account the communication cost to send data to the subplan examined for imbalance, and state is recreated (type A1 of assessment combined with type R1 of response); and (iii) when the *Diagnoser* does take into account the communication cost to send data to the subplan examined for imbalance, and no state is recreated (type A2 of assessment combined with type R2 of response). In essence, when the communication cost is not considered (assessment A1), an assumption is made that the cost for sending data overlaps with the cost of processing data due to pipelined parallelism. We believe that such an assumption is valid for this specific experiment, and indeed, this is verified by the experimental results discussed next.

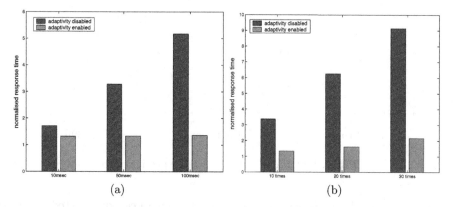

Fig. 3. (a) Performance of Q2 for retrospective adaptations; (b) performance of Q1 for prospective adaptations and double data size

The performance of the three configurations for Q1 is shown in Fig. 2(b). Although all of them result in significant gains compared to the static system, some perform better than others. From this figure we can observe: (i) that taking pipelining into consideration (by performing the assessment of type A1) has an impact on the quality of the decisions and results in better repartitioning (see the difference between the leftmost and the rightmost bar in each group); and (ii) that retrospective adaptations (R1 response) behave better than the prospective ones for bigger perturbations (see the difference between the leftmost and the middle bar in each group). The latter is also expected, as the overhead for recreating state remains stable independently of the size of perturbations, whereas the benefits of removing tuples already sent to the slower consumers, and resending them to the faster ones increases for bigger perturbations. Also, from Fig. 2(b), it can been seen that the bars referring to retrospective adaptations remain similar with different sizes of perturbation, which means that the size of performance improvements increases with the size of perturbations. This happens for two complementary reasons: (i) the higher the perturbation, the more tuples are evaluated by the faster machine, in a way that outweighs the increased overhead for redistributing tuples already sent or buffered to be sent; and (ii) for any of these perturbations, only a very small portion of the tuples is evaluated by the slower machine, which makes the performance of the system less sensitive to the size of perturbation of this machine.

Experiments with Q2 lead to the same conclusions. Fig. 3(a) shows the behaviour of the join query when the *sleep()* process sleeps for 10, 50 and 100 msecs, respectively, and adaptations are of type A1 of assessment and R1 of response. As already identified in Fig. 2(b), retrospective adaptations are characterised by better scalability, and their performance is less dependent on the perturbation.

Varying the dataset size. From the figures presented up to this point, retrospective adaptations outperform the prospective ones, but suffer from higher overhead. The reason why prospective adaptations exhibit worse performance

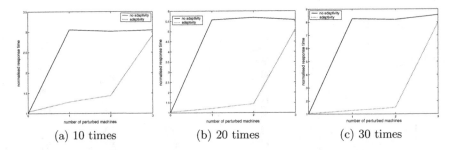

(a) 10 times	(b) 20 times	(c) 30 times

Fig. 4. Performance of Q1 for retrospective adaptations

is that a significant proportion of the tuples have been distributed before the adaptations can take place. Intuitively, this can be mitigated in larger queries. Indeed, this is verified by increasing the dataset size of Q1 from 3000 tuples to 6000, and making one WS call 10, 20 and 30 times costlier than the other, and the adaptations are prospective. Fig. 3(b) shows the results, which are very close to those when adaptations are retrospective (i.e., Fig. 2(b) for Q1 and Fig. 3(a) for Q2 compared to Fig. 2(a)), and lead to better performance improvements.

Varying the number of perturbed machines. Fig. 4 complements the above remarks by showing the performance of Q1 for different numbers of perturbed machines when adaptations are retrospective (three machines have been used for WS evaluation in this experiment). Again, perturbations are inserted by making one WS call 10, 20 and 30 times costlier than the other (Fig. 4(a), (b) and (c), respectively). Due to the dynamic balancing property, the performance degrades very gracefully in the presence of perturbed machines. As explained in detail earlier, the performance when adaptivity is enabled, is very similar for different magnitudes of perturbation, when there is at least one unperturbed machine. Thus the plots corresponding to the case of enabled adaptivity are similar for up to two out of three perturbed machines. Note that the relative degradation (i.e., difference from value 1 in the figures) can be improved by an order of magnitude.

Overheads. This set of experiments investigates overheads. We run Q1 when there is no WS perturbation. As shown from Table 1, the overhead of prospective adaptations is 5.9%. This value is the average of two cases. When the adaptivity mechanism is enabled but no actual redistribution takes place, the overhead is 6.2%. However, due to slight fluctuations in performance that are inevitable in a real wide-area environment, if the query is relatively long-running, the system may adapt even though the WSs are the same. For prospective adaptations, a poor initial redistribution may have detrimental effects, since by the time the system realises that there was no need for adaptation, the stored tuples may already have been sent to their destination. Nevertheless, on average, the system behaves reasonably with respect to small changes in performance and incurs a 5.6% overhead. The ratio of the number of tuples sent to the two machines is

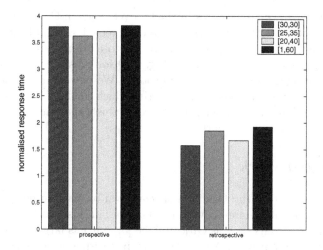

Fig. 5. Performance of Q1 under changing perturbations

slightly imbalanced: 1.21. The overhead is slightly smaller than when no actual redistribution occurs as there are benefits from the redistribution.

When the adaptations are retrospective, the overhead is significantly higher, as already discussed. However, the ratio of the tuples is close to the one indicating perfect balance: 1.01. From the above, it can be concluded that retrospective adaptations, even if they are not necessary for ensuring correctness, may be employed when perturbations are large. However, it is felt that the overheads imposed for both types of distribution are reasonable and are worthwhile given the scale of expected gains during perturbations.

We also examined the behaviour of the system for Q1, when the WS cost on one machine is 10 times greater than on the other, and the frequency of generating raw monitoring events from the query engine varies between 0 (i.e., no monitoring to drive adaptivity), and 1 notification per 10, 20 and 30 tuples produced. Both the adaptation quality and the overhead incurred were rather insensitive to these monitoring frequencies (figure omitted due to space limitations). This is because (i) the mechanism to produce low-level monitoring notifications has been shown to have very low overhead [10], and (ii) the adaptivity components filter the notifications effectively. On average, between 100 and 300 notifications are generated from the query engine, but the *MonitoringEventDetector* needs to notify the *Diagnoser* only around 10 times, 1-3 of which lead to actual rebalancing. Thus the system is not flooded by messages, which keeps the overhead low.

Rapid Changes. The final set of experiments aims to show the dynamic nature of the system. Thus far, the perturbations have been stable throughout execution. A question arises as to whether the system can exhibit similar performance gains when perturbations vary in magnitude over the lifetime of the run. In these experiments the perturbation varies for each incoming tuple in a normally distributed way, so that the mean value remains stable. Fig. 5 shows the results when the differences in the two WS costs in Q1 vary between 25 and 35 times, between 20 and 40 times, and between 1 and 60 times The leftmost bar in each group in the figure corresponds to a stable cost, which is 30 times higher (e.g., bar A1-R2, 30times in Fig. 2(b) for prospective adaptations), and is presented again for comparison purposes. We can see that the performance with adaptivity is modified only slightly, which enables us to claim that the approach to dynamic balancing proposed in this paper can adapt efficiently to rapid changes of resource performance.

4   Related Work

Query processing on the Grid is a special form of distributed query processing over wide-area autonomous environments. Work in this area has resulted in many interesting proposals such as ObjectGlobe [5], but has largely ignored the issues of intra-query adaptivity. Adaptive query processing is an active research area [4]. However, proposals usually focus on centralised, mostly single-node query processing, and do not yet provide robust mechanisms for responding to changes in the resource performance, which is important especially when an arbitrarily large number of autonomous resources can participate in the query execution, as it is the case in Grid query processing.

As an example that does consider distributed settings, [14] deals with adaptations to changing statistics of data from remote sources, whereas our proposal, complementarily, focuses on changing resource behaviour. Moreover, sources in [14] only provide data, and do not otherwise contribute to the query evaluation, which takes place centrally. Eddies [3] are also used in centralised processing of data streams to adapt to changing data characteristics (e.g., [6]) and operator consumption speeds. When Eddies are distributed, as in [19], such consumption speeds may indicate changing resources. Nevertheless, our approach is more generic as (i) it is not clear how distributed Eddies [19] can extract the statistics they need in a wide-area environment, and how they can keep the messaging overhead low; (ii) Eddies cannot handle all kinds of physical operators (e.g., traditional hash joins); and (iii) redistribution of operator state is not supported. Adapting to changing data properties has also been considered in distributed query processing over streams [8].

In general, workload balancing has been thoroughly examined in parallel databases, but only assuming a context where participating machines either share resources such as disks and memory, or are inter-connected by fast dedicated networks in such a way that data communication is simple and not expensive. As OGSA-DQP is deployed in a different setting, the infrastructure for traditional workload balancing needs to be revisited. For data and state repartitioning, the most relevant work is the Flux operator for continuous queries [17]. The Flux approach has been implemented at the operator level, whereas, our approach is based on loosely coupled components, which can be more easily extended. Rivers [2] follow a simpler approach, and are capable of performing data (but not state) repartitioning. State management has also been considered in [9], but only with a view to allowing more efficient, adaptive tuple rerouting within a single-node query plan.

5   Conclusions

The volatility of the environment in parallel query processing over heterogeneous and autonomous wide-area resources makes it imperative to adapt to changing resource performance, in order not to suffer from serious performance degradation. This paper proposes a solution for dynamic workload balancing through data and operator state repartitioning. This solution is instantiated in the context of a more generic architectural framework implemented through extensions to the Grid-enabled open-source OGSA-DQP system. The implementation is particularly appealing for environments such as the Grid, as it is based on loosely-coupled components, engineered as Grid Services, which communicate asynchronously and support the publish/subscribe model. The results of the empirical evaluation are promising: performance is significantly improved (by an order of magnitude in some cases), while the overhead remains low enough to allow the benefits of adaptation to outweigh the cost in a wide range of scenarios.

Acknowledgements. This work has been supported by the UK EPSRC grant GR/R51797/01, and by the UK e-Science Programme through the DAIT project.

References

1. N. Alpdemir, A. Mukherjee, A. Gounaris, N. W. Paton, P. Watson, and A. A. A. Fernandes. OGSA-DQP: A grid service for distributed querying on the grid. In *Proc. of 9th EDBT Conference*, pages 858–861, 2004.
2. R. Arpaci-Dusseau, E. Anderson, N. Treuhaft, D. Culler, J. Hellerstein, D. Patterson, and K. Yelick. Cluster I/O with River: Making the fast case common. In *Proc. of the Sixth IOPADS Workshop*, pages 10–22, 1999.
3. R. Avnur and J. Hellerstein. Eddies: continuously adaptive query processing. In *Proc. of ACM SIGMOD 2000*, pages 261–272, 2000.
4. S. Babu and P. Bizarro. Adaptive query processing in the looking glass. In *CIDR*, pages 238–249, 2005.
5. R. Braumandl, M. Keidl, A. Kemper, K. Kossmann, A. Kreutz, S. Seltzsam, and K. Stocker. ObjectGlobe: Ubiquitous query processing on the Internet. *VLDB Journal*, 10(1):48–71, Aug. 2001.
6. S. Chandrasekaran and M. Franklin. PSoup: a system for streaming queries over streaming data. *VLDB Journal*, 12:140–156, 2003.
7. S. Chaudhuri, V. Narasayya, and R. Ramamurthy. Estimating progress of execution for sql queries. In *Proc. of ACM SIGMOD*, pages 803–814, 2004.
8. M. Cherniack, H. Balakrishnan, M. Balazinska, D. Carney, U. Cetintemel, Y. Xing, and S. Zdonik. Scalable distributed stream processing. In *CIDR*, 2003.
9. A. Deshpande and J. M. Hellerstein. Lifting the burden of history from adaptive query processing. *Proc. of 30th VLDB Conf.*, pages 948–959, 2004.

10. A. Gounaris, N. W. Paton, A. A. A. Fernandes, and R. Sakellariou. Self monitoring query execution for adaptive query processing. *Data and Knowledge Engineering*, 51(3):325–348, 2004.

11. A. Gounaris, R. Sakellariou, N. W. Paton, and A. A. A.Fernandes. Resource scheduling for parallel query processing on computational grids. In *Proc. of 5th IEEE/ACM GRID Workshop*, pages 396–401, 2004.

12. G. Graefe. Encapsulation of parallelism in the Volcano query processing system. In *Proc. of ACM SIGMOD*, pages 102–111, 1990.

13. G. Graefe. Query evaluation techniques for large databases. *ACM Computing Surveys*, 25(2):73–170, 1993.

14. Z. Ives, A. Halevy, and D. Weld. Adapting to source properties in processing data integration queries. In *Proc. of ACM SIGMOD*, pages 395–406, 2004.

15. D. Kossmann. The state of the art in distributed query processing. *ACM Computing Surveys*, 32(4):422–469, 2000.

16. D. T. Liu, M. J. Franklin, and D. Parekh. GridDB: a relational interface for the grid. In *Proc. of ACM SIGMOD*, pages 660–660, 2003.

17. M. Shah, J. Hellerstein, S. Chandrasekaran, and M. Franklin. Flux: An adaptive partitioning operator for continuous query systems. In *Proc. of ICDE*, pages 25–36, 2003.

18. J. Smith and P. Watson. Fault-tolerance in distributed query processing. Technical Report CS-TR-893, School of Computing Science, The University of Newcastle upon Tyne, 2004.

19. F. Tian and D. DeWitt. Tuple routing strategies for distributed eddies. In *Proc. of 29th VLDB Conference*, pages 333–344, 2003.

An Adaptive Distributed Query Processing Grid Service

Fabio Porto[1], Vinícius F.V. da Silva[2], Márcio L. Dutra[2,3], and Bruno Schulze[2]

[1] EPFL - School of Computer and Communication Sciences,
Database Laboratory, Lausanne, Switzerland
fabio.porto@epfl.ch

[2] National Laboratory for Scientific Computation - Computer Science Dep,
RJ - Brazil

[3] Military Institute of Engineering - System Engineering Dep, RJ - Brazil

Abstract. Grid services provide an important abstract layer on top of heterogeneous components (hardware and software) that take part into a grid environment. We are developing a data grid service prototype that aims at providing transparent use of grid resources to data intensive scientific applications. Our prototype was designed having as target three main issues: (1) dynamic scheduling and allocation of query execution engine modules into grid nodes; (2)adaptability of query execution to variations on environment conditions and (3) support to special scientific operations. We propose a new node scheduling algorithm and show how it can be integrated into a simple distributed and parallel query optimization strategy. Our implementation demonstrates a speedup of 16.6 with 18 scheduled nodes and a steady throughput rate, obtained applying a dynamic adaptive strategy.

1 Introduction

The development of grid services as proposed by the Open Grid Services Architecture OGSA [1] promotes the isolation of user applications in respect to the heterogeneity inherent to the grid environment. While middleware systems like the Globus toolkit [2] offer some basic functionalities on top of a grid infrastructure, mainly regarding: authentication, remote task scheduling and file transfer, this is not enough for the deployment of complex applications involving the processing of users programs and the access to distributed data. For these more complex types of applications an extension was proposed of the web service technology towards (grid) web services, where services state and life cycle can be managed [3]. This extension was first proposed in the OGSI - Open Grid Services Infrastructure and more recently has been turned into the WSRF Web Services Resource Framework [3]. The idea is that by designing and composing grid services, one may achieve higher level functionalities specific tailored to the envisaged application and still support the fundamental characteristics offered by established distributed systems such as Common Request Broker Architecture CORBA, from the Object Management Group. Regarding data services for

J.-M. Pierson (Ed.): VLDB DMG 2005, LNCS 3836, pp. 45–57, 2005.

the grid, some projects like OGSA-DAI [4] and Data Grid [5] aim at providing a uniform service interface for data access and integration of databases in the grid, in addition to higher-level services like data replication.

Our project contributes to the grid data service layer by conceiving high-level services for data intensive grid applications. In this context, we are developing a Configurable Data Integration Middleware for the grid (CoDIMS-G) that is a distributed grid service for the evaluation of scientific queries. The design of CoDIMS-G focused on conceiving efficient and adaptable query evaluation strategies for the grid environment. Efficiency comes with adequate initial resource allocation based on grid nodes historical profiles and managing inter-node communication. Adaptability is the result of online routing decisions and transfer block size management.

We designed a query optimization strategy tailored for queries including intensive computations, like scientific programs. The strategy integrates a new node scheduling algorithm that selects grid nodes for parallel evaluation of fragments of the query execution plan. In addition, we implemented a distributed query engine, running as grid services, that adapts execution to the actual data flow in allocated grid nodes. We extended the Eddy operator [6] to deal with the adaptivity of tuple block size routing through scheduled nodes and to implement an iteration mechanism over a query execution plan fragment, as required by loop control found in some scientific applications.

We currently use CoDIMS-G to support the pre-processing stage of a scientific visualization application (SVA)that is being developed at the National Laboratory of Scientific Computing (LNCC), in Brazil, as a testbed for our prototype. The SVA computes the path of virtual particles through a fluid flow [7]. Our challenge is to minimize the elapsed-time for pre-computing the virtual particle trajectory. We modelled this scenario as a database problem and used CoDIMS-G to generate and evaluate a parallel query execution plan that transparently access grid resources and dynamically adapt to unforeseen fluctuations during query execution.

Our implementation demonstrates a speedup of 16.6 [1] with 18 scheduled nodes and a steady throughput rate.

The rest of this paper is organized as follows. In section 2, we present important work covering grid data services and scientific visualization. Next, section 3 introduces our running example based on the pre-processing stage of fluid path visualization. Section 4 introduces the CODIMS-G architecture and section 5 presents the distributed query optimization strategy. Emphasis is given on the G^2N scheduling algorithm and its integration into the query execution plan. Section 6 presents the query execution engine components and discuss the influence of our distributed adaptive strategy into query execution. Section 7 presents initial results obtained running CoDIMS-G in a controlled environment with up to 20 grid nodes. Finally, we present our conclusions and future work.

---

[1] We computed speedup as the ratio between the elapsed-time of a centralized execution and a parallel one.

2   Related Work

The problem of integrating distributed query processing technology with a grid service has been addressed in the OGSA-DQP project [8]. In this project, the query processor is served by a set of orchestrated services that manage distributed data access, resources metadata information and services instances creation and management. The DQP service is built on top of a OGSA-DAI [9] implementation that provides services interfaces for data source access; data transfer and data source services instances management. Query processing is done by services encapsulating the Polar* [10] distributed object oriented query processor. DQP offers query capabilities very similar to those proposed in this paper. Query execution service instances are deployed in grid nodes to implement user programs parallelization. Physical algebraic operators, like exchange and operation-call, implement inter-node communication and user program invocations, respectively. Our proposal differs from the one in OGSA-DQP in the following aspects. Firstly, we propose a grid node selection algorithm based on historical of application execution and integrate it into a distributed query optimization strategy. Secondly, in contrast to DQP static generated query execution plan, our query execution engine extends Eddies adaptive query execution strategy to cope with execution time variations not captured during query optimization stage. Finally, we dynamically reanalyze node allocation by comparing actual node throughput with estimated values and, eventually, calling the dynamic optimizer to reschedule grid nodes.

There has also been some work on adaptive execution of applications in the grid environment [11]. These works focus on adapting the execution of an application to the changing conditions of selected grid nodes. The problem in this context is to identify points where execution may be interrupted in a node and restarted in other nodes, keeping data context. In respect to CoDIMS-G approach, these would be classified as application centric adaptations, whereas CoDIMS-G is data centric adaptation, managing adaptation in the tuple/block level.

Examples of scientific visualization applications problems that consider particles tracing problems can be found in [16]. Such problem can be mathematically defined by an initial value problem [12]: dx /dt = F(x,t), x(0)=P0, (1) where $F : R3 \ x \ R + \ - > R$, is a time-dependent vector field (velocity, for example). The solution of problem (1) for a set of initial conditions gives a set of integral curves which can be interpreted as the trajectory of massless particles upon the flow defined by the field F(x,t). Other particle tracing methods can be used (streamlines, streaklines, among others.) with slight modifications of the above equation [13].

3   The Scientific Visualization Problem

We use as testbed application, the preprocessing stage of scientific visualization application that simulates a fluid flow through a path [7]. In this preprocessing stage, an instant shot of the flow is taken and comprises a set of fluid virtual particles (VP), and a geometry model of the domain, with velocity vectors associated to space objects. In addition, two user programs are involved.

The database representation for the pre-computing stage of the scientific visualization application we are using comprehends the relations: *Geometry, Velocity* and *Particle* and two user programs. The *Geometry* relation stores data associated with polyhedron's geometry and the *Velocity* relation corresponds to velocity vectors for each time instant, whereas the *Particle* relation holds the initial particle position. The *Resulting-vector* user program computes a resulting speed vector in a specific position of the flow path and the Trajectory Computing Program (TCP) computes VP's subsequent position, given its initial position and the corresponding resulting speed vector. The database model for this application is represented below[2]:

relation schema:

- Geometry (idpolyhedron integer, polyhedron list of $<$ *pointid integer, vertice point* $>$)
- Velocity (idpolyhedron integer,timeinstant integer, speed-vector list of $<$ *point* $>$)
- Particle (part-id integer,position point)

user programs interface:

- Resulting-vector(point, speed-vector list of $<$ *point* $>$): point;
- TCP (point, speed):new-position.

The computation of each particle iteration can be expressed with an SQL query, such as the one in Figure 1.

```
Select part.part-id, TCP(part.position,resulting-vector(part.position,v.speed-vector))
From g in geometry, v in velocity,
     part in particle
Where part.position in g.polyhedron and
    g.idpolyhedron = v.idpolyhedron and
    v.timeinstant = $time
```

Fig. 1. TCP query

Some aspects of this model require special attention. The trajectory of a virtual particle through the fluid path is simulated by a certain number of intermediary positions, between the initial and final position of the virtual particle in the path, referred to as *iterations* in the SVA jargon. Usually, higher number of iterations accounts for a smoother visualization of virtual particles flow. Computing intermediary positions in the path corresponds, in our database model, to repetitively computing the TCP query with different *time* values and initial

---

[2] We consider an Object-Relational model [14].

position for each virtual particle. Regarding the respective query execution plan, iterations correspond to multiple evaluations of a single query execution plan fragment. Secondly, the join predicate between *Particle* and *Geometry* relations is modelled as a spatial join [15] where the position of a particle matches the region defined by the polyhedron.

Such queries can take a long time to process on conventional machines as a result of: the number of particles; the number of iterations; the size of the geometry; the hash-join swap profile or/and the fluid path model complexity. As a result of this, using the processing power available in a grid environment may substantially reduce the time needed for pre-processing virtual particle trajectory. Nevertheless, in order to make it feasible for the scientific visualization community, one must provide services that will hide the complexity of executing a query, like the one in Figure 1, in a grid environment.

Therefore, CoDIMS-G offers transparent data access with integrated user's programs execution within the grid. It is designed to offer efficient, adaptive and high level query processing service for scientific applications.

4   CoDIMS-G Architecture

CoDIMS-G is an instance of the CoDIMS environment [16] that is being developed to support data and program integration for scientific applications running in a grid. The main components of the CoDIMS-G architecture are depicted in Figure 2.

The entry point for user query submission is provided as a service running in a gatekeeper machine accessible both from outside and inside of the grid. Users requests are forwarded to the Control component, which sends them to

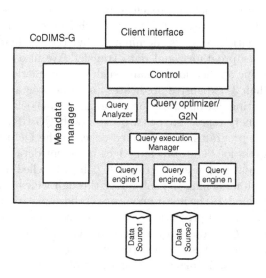

Fig. 2. The CoDIMS-G architecture

the query processing system. The latter is composed of: a query analyzer; a query optimizer; a query execution manager and query engines (QE). The query optimizer includes a scheduler component that selects available nodes to be used during query execution. In particular, whenever an algebraic operator is parallelized, the scheduler indicates the set of interesting nodes to be allocated for its evaluation. The scheduler and optimizer cooperate to generate an initial distributed parallel query execution plan $DQEP$. A QE is the component where actual query execution takes place. It creates the physical operators conforming to the $DQEP$, including data process and control flow operators. Instances of QE are instantiated into grid scheduled nodes. Each QE receives a fragment of the $DQEP$ and is responsible for the instantiation of the operators and the execution control, including the communication with other fragments for tuple consumption and production. As part of the $DQEP$, the scan operator accesses data sources using wrappers that prepare the data according to a global data model.

5   Distributed Query Processing

In this section we describe the grid query optimization strategy adopted in CoDIMS-G.

Considering the lack of and fluctuation on grid resources statistics, and the particularities of some scientific data sources, a static query execution plan can be highly inefficient. As such, we opted for a simple query optimization strategy that produces an initial, not necessarily optimal, $DQEP$ that will be adapted during execution. Adaptation in this context, stems for the fact that tuple routing is decided based on actual performance measures obtained from running operators or allocated nodes.

Our query optimization approach is inspired on the SystemR* distributed query optimization strategy [17]. The approach focuses on distributed queries in which the execution cost is dominated by the evaluation of: expensive predicates [3], user programs, and data transfer. We also explore a particularity of the scientific application domain, such as that queries usually include few (rarely more than 3) expensive predicates and user programs.

Before presenting our optimization algorithm, some definitions are necessary. We consider a query represented as a query graph QG [18], where nodes model relations or user programs. Non directed edges in the QG represent join predicates between relations and directed edges represent data dependency between nodes (eg. an input to a user program). A pair of labelled directed edges determine a sub-graph modelling the sub-query through which tuples should iterate. This is to accommodate the iteration nature of the application we are supporting. Finally, restrictions and projections are annotated with corresponding nodes.

Based on the QG produced by a query analyzer and in accordance to its data dependency and query restrictions, the query optimization algorithm explores the search space of valid plans. The analyzes of the search space is conducted

---

[3] Joins and predicates over user program results.

according to two principles: obeyance to the sub-query iteration borders; focus on expensive predicate evaluation order and definition of a parallelization strategy for expensive operators. The challenge is to come up with a simple strategy (i.e. one that consumes a very small fraction of query elapsed-time) that accommodates all these principles. In view of this, the adopted query optimization approach explores all valid execution orders of expensive predicates in QG nodes. For each expensive operator in a plan, a decision must be made regarding the use of grid resources to run it in a intra-operator parallel mode. Three alternatives are analyzed: (a)non parallelization, (b)scheduling according to the G^2N algorithm (see section 5.1), and (c) adoption of the same parallelization strategy used by the previous operator in the query execution plan. For each computed query execution plan, a cost is associated, using a parallel pipeline cost function [19]. The $DQEP$ presenting the lowest cost is selected for execution.

Additionally, the query optimizer introduces into the $DQEP$ transfer operators, Sender (Receiver) and Split(Merge). These operators are placed in the borders of data transfer between nodes. Moreover, the Eddy operator is placed in the $DQEP$ in the base of an iteration fragment. Note that, in our implementation, Eddy responds for the iteration of tuples through a sub-query.

The initial $DQEP$ is the basis for the correct instantiation of query operators during query execution phase. It gives the correct data processing semantics and control flow operators necessary for an equivalent execution in respect to a user query. As we will present in section 6, the actual routing of tuple evaluation is defined by the Eddy operator based on runtime characteristics and restrictions specified in the $DQEP$.

5.1   The Grid Greedy Node Scheduling Algorithm

In this section we present the grid greedy node G^2N scheduling algorithm. The main idea behind G^2N can be stated as: "an optimal parallel allocation strategy for an independent query operator, of a tuple by tuple type, in a set of nodes is the one in which the operator execution elapsed-time is minimum with respect to the evaluation of a bag of tuples and produces a balanced use of resources".

The problem can be formalized as follows: given a set of N nodes, with information regarding node throughput, and a set of equally costly independent tasks P, define a subset N_1 of N, which minimizes the elapsed-time for evaluating all tasks in P.

The G^2N algorithm receives a set of available nodes with corresponding average throughput $(tp_1, tp_2, \ldots, tp_n)$, measured in tuples per second. This includes the average cost involved in transferring one tuple to the evaluating node and processing it. The output of G^2N comprises a set of selected grid nodes. We now briefly present a description of the algorithm. Initially, the algorithm classifies the list of available grid nodes in decreasing order of their corresponding average throughput values. It then allocates all T tuples to the fastest node. The main program loop tries to reallocate, at least one tuple from the already allocated nodes to a new grid node (less performing, next in line). Tuples are extracted from a node representing the highest elapsed-time so far. If it succeeds to do so, by producing a new evaluation estimation with reduced query elapsed-time, it continues reallocating tuples to the new allocated grid node, until the overall elapsed-time becomes higher than the last computed one. Conversely, if the reallocation of a single tuple produces an execution with higher elapsed-time than the one without the new grid node, the algorithm stops and outputs the grid nodes accepted so far.

The output produced by G^2N loads the query optimizer with parallelization decision regarding each expensive operator, adding to the generation of the initial query execution plan and the re-scheduling of allocated nodes in face of variations on estimated values.

Summarizing this section, we discussed the optimization strategy adopted in CoDIMS-G for generating an initial distributed query execution plan for queries similar to the one in Figure 1. Once the $DQEP$ has been produced it is sent to the query execution machine for evaluation. The execution process is described in section 6.

6   Query Execution

Query execution in $CoDIMS$-G is implemented as an instance of the $QEEF$ [20] software framework, designed to allow extensions to support new query characteristics, including new operators, different query algebra and execution models among others.

The distributed query engine architecture comprises a distribution node, running the Eddy operator and remote QE nodes, running fragments of the $DQEP$, Figure 3. Rectangles in figure 3 correspond to $DQEP$ operator fragments and edges represent data flow.

The eddy operator consumes tuples from query data-sources and routes them in tuple block unit to remote nodes running a fragment of the $DQEP$. Once tuples reach the top of the remote fragment, they are again packed into a tuple block and bounced back to eddy. For a given tuple, this cycle continues until it is eliminated by a restriction operation or it has been processed by all operations and passed through all iterations in the $DQEP$.

Our eddy implementation includes a pair of split/send operators, that distributes tuples to QEs running remote fragments and receive/merge that obtains tuples evaluated by remote fragments. The split and merge operators compose the distribution function of eddy. The sender operator allocates tuples to be transferred to nodes according to a block size computed as a function of the target node throughput, the number of tuples allocated to the node by G^2N and the communication cost. As a matter of fact, as we have observed in our experimentation, the block size has a large influence in the whole eddy throughput.

It is a unit for managing system adaptivity. The split operator modifies a remote node block size in the following scenarios. Firstly, in the event of a timeout. The sender controls the limit of time it waits for completing a block. The timeout value is computed as a function of the expected time to evaluate a block

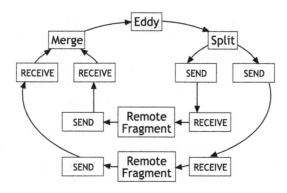

Fig. 3. CoDIMS-G adaptive query execution framework

of tuples. If a timeout is reached, the block is sent with the current number of allocated tuples. Secondly, eddy proceeds a local adaptation by checking on current throughput values registered for a node. If average throughput shows differences of 30% in respect to estimated values, eddy re-computes the node block size with a variation corresponding to the throughput one. Thirdly, eddy checks on global variations [4] concerning all scheduled nodes. When the average variation crosses a threshold, eddy invokes G^2N and proceeds a re-scheduling of nodes.

Data requests from competing remote fragments are prioritized in a queue by the split operator that produces one block of tuples a time with block size corresponding to that of the highest throughput node requesting data to be consumed.

6.1   Supporting Scientific Applications

In order to support the SVA, the *QEEF* framework has been extended to cope with the following requirements: user's program execution; spatial and temporal hash-joins; loop control over query execution plan fragment; distribution and parallelism. The strategy for introducing user programs into a *DQEP* is to implement the Apply operator [21] as a new algebraic operator that encapsulates users' program invocation and parameters passing by values extracted from input tuples. The operator implements the standard iterator interface [22] and, for each tuple, invokes the user program with the input parameters captured from the input tuple. User program's result is concatenated to the input tuple to compose an output tuple.

The SVA required the design and implementation of a spatial-hash join (SHJ) operator. As other operators, the SHJ implements the iterator interface. The operator was implemented with two main modules:partition and probe, each running in different threads. The partition module consumes tuples placing them

---

[4] Global variations are computed comparing estimated throughput values and actual values for each node and taking the average.

in buckets according to their position. Next, the probe thread load buckets and evaluate joins. The choice of the hash-join algorithm is based on the fact that the geometry data will usually not fit in main memory and a nice partitioning function may distribute tetrahedrons into buckets according to the path followed by the fluid, reducing the number of IOs [5]. The parallelization strategy adopted for hash-joins considers that all instances of the join operator receive the complete geometry data, so that particles distribution is independent of the hash-join instance and can be scheduled according to node performance measures. Such decision eliminates the restriction regarding G^2N for this problem, allowing the same scheduling function to be used during optimization. The overhead of transferring the complete geometry data to scheduled node is reduced by adopting a *multicast* transfer protocol approach [23].

Another nice property of the eddy operator, not previously observed in the literature regards its natural loop execution model. Some scientific applications, like the SVA, require a fragment of the *DQEP* to be repetitively evaluated. In our running example, the TCP query has to be run for each single iteration of a virtual particle. The looping execution model of Eddy adapts nicely to the repetitive evaluation of query execution plan fragments.

7   Initial Results

In this section we report on initial experimental results. We have implemented CoDIMS-G using java 1.4.2 and globus 3.2.1 with the OGSA container. We simulated a grid environment into a cluster with 20 pentium IV, 1.7 GHz, processors with 256 MB of RAM, running linux 2.4.20-31.9.

We used a real set of data from a SVA produced at LNCC by visualization scientists. We considered an instance of the SVA problems with 1000 particles and executing 25 iterations by each particle. The geometry data source comprises 71732 tetrahedrons and the velocity relation holds 25 time-instant values for each geometry vertex. The TCP and Resulting-vector programs have been ported to java and the spatial hash-join algorithm has been added to the QEEF framework.

We analyzed the elapsed-time of executing the query in figure 1, obtained by increasing the number of nodes in 4 steps, from 1 node to 18 nodes, see Figure 4(b). Figures correspond to averaging the results of 10 runs in each step. The elapsed-time considers the difference between the time instant eddy finishes its evaluation (i.e. executes the close request) and the time it receives the *open* request from query manager. Results demonstrated a speedup of 16.6 with 18 nodes. Another interesting observation is that the projection of G^2N is accurate. The ratio between the elapsed-time obtained during execution and the one projected by G^2N shows differences of only 0.1, which reinforces the proposed scheduling algorithm.

Figure 4(a) presents the system throughput during execution. Each point in the graph corresponds to the number of tuples evaluated by eddy so far (x

---

[5] We have not yet adapted the partitioning function to benefit from data characteristics, such as the fluid flow.

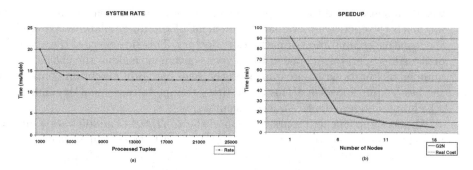

Fig. 4. Experimental results

axe), divided by the current elapsed-time (y axe). We obtained a steady average throughput of 4.54 tuples per second, after 1/3 tuples have been evaluated by eddy. In fact, we observed that the initial disturb was due to one of the nodes that took longer, 2.3 cycles, to behave as expected. More interesting is to recognize that our system was able to recover from this initial problem and to achieve the projected throughput.

8   Conclusion

The vision of providing transparent and automated access to and use of a large number of heterogeneous hardware and software resources available in the internet and intranets has motivated efforts towards the development of grid environments. To this end the Global Grid Forum has supported the *OGSA* architecture, based on a service-oriented technology, that addresses the need for standardization regarding grid component discovery, access, allocation, execution, monitoring , among others.

Scientific applications are natural candidates for benefiting from a grid environment as a result of: the large amount of data to be processed; the distribution of scientific resources, in terms of human, hardware and software and high computing power requirements.

In this paper we presented the *CoDIMS-G*, which is an adaptive distributed query processing grid service. *CODIMS-G* offers users a transparent object-relational view over data and programs distributed in the internet through a set of orchestrated services.

We propose a new dynamic grid node allocation algorithm based on node throughput, and integrate it into a simple query optimization strategy that generates initial query execution plans with annotated node scheduling policy. The proposed query execution strategy extends *eddy* adaptive query execution model for the grid environment. The combination of both, simple query optimization with node scheduling and adaptive query execution model, offers a very convenient platform for query execution in a grid environment, considering the variations on grid nodes run-time conditions and the lack of statistics from the web data-sources and the user programs execution. In addition, we use the eddy approach to repetitively evaluate a fragment of the query plan, as required by the iterative computation of particles trajectory. This side effect of the adoption of the eddy operator happened to be very convenient making the choice on the number of iterations to be transparently dealt by eddy execution control. To the best of our knowledge, this is the first attempt to combine a dynamic node scheduling and an adaptive query execution.

We have implemented a first version of the *CoDIMS-G* middleware. Our implementation demonstrates a speedup of 16.6 with 18 scheduled nodes and a steady throughput rate of 4.5 tuples per second, obtained once the system recovered from initial disturbs applying our adaptive strategy.

As future work, we intend to further investigate the correlation among block size, node throughput and volume of tuples in eddy. We also plan to evaluate the spatial hash-join algorithm, under scenarios where buckets swap are minimized as function of the data being joined.

References

1. Foster, I., Kesselman, C., Nick, J., Tuecke, S.: The Physiology of the Grid: An Open Grid Services Architecture for Distributed System integration. Global Grid Forum (2002)
2. Foster, I., Kesselman, C.: Globus a metacomputing infrastructure toolkit". Intl. Journal Supercomputer Applications **11** (1997) 115–128
3. Czajkowski, K., et al.: From open grid services infrastructure to wsresource framework: Refactoring & evolution, version 1.1. Technical report, http://www.globus.org/wsrf/specs/ogsitowsrf1.0.pdf (2005)
4. Antonioletti, M., Atkinsons, M., et all., A.B.: The design and implementation of grid database services in ogsa-dai. Concurrency and Computation: Practice and Experience Journal. **17** (2005) 357–376
5. Chervenak, A., Foster, I., Kesselman, C., Salisbury, C., Tuecke, S.: The data grid: Towards an architecture for the distributed management and analysis of large scientific datasets (1999)
6. Avnur, R., Hellerstein., J.: Eddies: continuously adaptive query processing. ACM SIGMOD Record **29** (2000) 261–272
7. Porto, F., Giraldi, G., de Oliveira, J.C., Schulze, B.: Codims - an adaptable middleware system for scientific visualization in grids. Concurrency and Computation: Practice and Experience Journal. **16** (2004) 515–522
8. Alpdemir, M.N., Mukherjee, A., Paton, N., et al.: Ogsa-dqp: A service-based distributed query processor for the grid. In J.Cox, S., ed.: Proc. of UK e-Science All Hands Meeting Nottingham. (2003)
9. Paton, N., Atkinson, M., Dialani, V., Pearson, D., T.Storey, P.Watson: Database access and integration services on the grid. Technical report, U.K. National eScience Center, www.nesc.ac.uk (2002)
10. Smith, J., Gounaris, A., Watson, P., Paton, N.W., et. al: Distributed query processing on the grid. LNCS 2536 (2002) 279–290
11. Vadhhiyar, S.S., Dongarra, J.J.: Self adaptivity in grid environment. Concurrency and Computation: Practice and Experience Journal. **17** (2005) 235–257

12. Rosenblum, L., et al., eds.: Scientific Visualization - Advances and Challenges. Academic Press (1994)
13. Barnard, S., et. al: Large-scale distributed computational fluid dynamics on the information power grid using globus. (1999) 60–67
14. Molina, H., Ullman, J.D., Widow, J.D.: Database Systems: The Complete Book. Prentice Hall (2001)
15. Lo, M.L., Ravishankar, C.V.: Spatial hash-joins. In: In Proc. of the ACM SIGMOD Conference on Management of Data, Montreal, Canada. (1996) 247–258
16. Barbosa, A., Porto, F., Melo, R.N.: Configurable data integration middleware system. Journal of the Brazilian Computer Society **8** (2002) 12–19
17. Selinger, P.G., Adiba, M.E.: Access path selections in distributed data base management systems. In: Proc. 1st Intl. Conf. on Databases, British Computer Society, Aberdeen. (1980)
18. Ozsu, M.T., Valduriez, P.: Principles of Distributed Database Systems. Prentice Hall International, Inc., New Jersey (1999)
19. Bouganim, L., Fabret, F., Porto, F., Valduriez., P.: Processing queries with expensive functions and large objects in distributed mediator systems. In: Proceedings of Int'l. Conf. on Data Engineering, Heidelberg, Germany (2001) 91–98
20. F. Ayres, F. Porto, R.N.M.: An extensible query execution engine for supporting new query execution models. Technical report, EPFL, Ecole Polytechnique Fdrale de Lausanne School of Computer and Communication Sciences, Suisse, *http : //icwww.epfl.ch/publications/documents/IC_TECH_REPORT_2005034.pdf* (2005)
21. Porto, F.: Strategies for the Parallel execution of user programs in scientific applications. PhD thesis, Pontifícia Universidade Católica do Rio de Janeiro, RJ, Brazil (2001)
22. Graefe, G.: Query evaluation techniques for large databases. ACM Computing Surveys **25** (1993) 73–170
23. Deering, S., Cheriton, D.: Multicast routing in datagram internetworks and extended lans. ACM Transactions on Computer Systems (**8**) 85–111

Framework for Querying Distributed Objects Managed by a Grid Infrastructure*

Ruslan Fomkin and Tore Risch

Department of Information Technology, Uppsala University,
P.O. Box 337, SE-751 05 Uppsala, Sweden
{Ruslan.Fomkin, Tore.Risch}@it.uu.se

Abstract. Queries over scientific data often imply expensive analyses of data requiring a lot of computational resources available in Grids. We are developing a customizable query processor built on top of an established Grid infrastructure, the NorduGrid middleware, and have implemented a framework for managing long running queries in Grid environment. With the framework the user does not specify the detailed job and parallelization descriptions required by NorduGrid. Instead s/he specifies queries in terms of an application-oriented schema describing contents of files managed by the Grid and accessed through wrappers. When a query is received by the system it generates NorduGrid job descriptions submitted to NorduGrid for execution. The framework considers limitations of NorduGrid. It includes a submission mechanism, a job babysitter, and a generic data exchange mechanism. The submission mechanism generates a number of jobs for parallel execution of a user query over wrapped data files. The task of the babysitter is to submit generated jobs to NorduGrid for the execution, to monitor their execution status, and to download results from the execution. The generic exchange mechanism provides a way to exchange objects through files between Grid execution nodes and user applications.

1 Introduction

Nowadays a lot of scientific data are stored in Grids. Scientists need to access and analyze them. Their analyses often imply expensive computations that need to process a lot of data. Thus scientists need to use external computational resources to process their analyses, and storage resources to store and share huge amounts of data. For this many Grids are developed to provide computational resources and storage facilities.

For example, the ATLAS collaboration [1] motivates many Grid projects such as LCG [2], EGEE [3], and NorduGrid [4]. These projects provide storage facilities to store and share data produced by ATLAS [1] and to be produced by the Large Hadron Collider (LHC) [5], along with computational resources to analyze the data.

---

* This work is funded by The Swedish Research Council (VR) under contract 343-2003-955.

J.-M. Pierson (Ed.): VLDB DMG 2005, LNCS 3836, pp. 58–70, 2005.

A typical analysis of data for the LHC projects is selections of subsets of the input data. The selections, called *cuts*, consist of not only simple logical predicates but also numerical computations. We show that such analyses can be expressed in a declarative way using an extensible query language.

We are developing *POQSEC* [6] (*Parallel Object Query System for Expensive Computations*) that processes scientific analyses specified as declarative SQL-like queries over data distributed in the Grid. It utilizes computational resources of Swegrid [7] and storage resources of Nordic countries through the middleware Grid infrastructure NorduGrid [4]. The goal of the POQSEC project is to provide a transparent and scalable way to specify and execute scientific queries. A user should be able to specify his/her query transparently in a client database without respect to where it will be executed and how data will be accessed.

Currently we have implemented a framework for submitting user queries for execution in the Grid. The system then creates jobs executing the queries, submits the jobs to NorduGrid, monitors execution of the jobs by NorduGrid, downloads results of the jobs, and delivers results of the queries to the user. The user states queries to POQSEC in terms of a database schema available in the client database. The schema contains both an application-oriented part and Grid meta-data. The application schema describes data stored inside files in Grid storage resources, for example events produced by ATLAS. Wrappers are defined for accessing the contents of these files, e.g. in our application we use a wrapper of the ROOT library [8]. The Grid meta-data contains information about the files. Thus user queries can restrict data both in terms of application data contents and meta-data about files. The latter is very important since there is a huge amount of Grid data files and queries are normally over a small percentage of them. User queries are parallelized to a number of jobs for execution. The parallelization is done by partitioning data between jobs. Our preliminary results show that the parallelization gives significant performance improvements.

The rest of the paper is organized as follows. Related work is discussed in Sect. 2. Section 3 describes the POQSEC architecture. It is followed by a description of an application from High Energy Physics, which is our test case. The implementation of the framework is discussed in Sect. 5, and Sect. 6 concludes the paper.

2 Related Work

Another system that utilizes a Grid infrastructure and provides high-level declarative query language for data access and analysis is Distributed Query Processing system (DQP) [9] or its web service version OGSA-DQP [10]. The DQP is part of the Grid infrastructure myGrid [11], which fully controls resources and where resources can be allocated dynamically. The resources for the query execution are allocated and provided by a user. Any of them can be utilized by DQP dynamically. It is different from our system where NorduGrid is a middleware above autonomous local batch systems that control computational resources. Unlike the DQP, we need to consider the NorduGrid limitation that jobs are not guaranteed to start immediately. Furthermore, as part of a job description NorduGrid requires to specify descriptions of resources in advance. This includes, for example, estimating execution time and number of computational nodes for jobs.

STORM [12] is a distributed query processing environment for processing selections over distributed large scientific datasets and transferring the selected data to its clients. STORM does not leverage an existing Grid infrastructure for data transportation, job scheduling, and batch query processing as POQSEC.

In [13,14] a batch database system is developed to support scientific queries. It is there applied on astronomical data. The data are stored in back-end SQL servers managed by a front-end batch query system. In POQSEC we use a middleware approach to access wrapped data stored in native format rather than storing the data in SQL databases.

ATLAS Distributed Analysis (ADA) [15] project has goal to provide high-level interface for scientists who analyze data produced by ATLAS and LHC. The users specify jobs containing datasets for processing in terms of meta-data and their analyses as snippets of programming code, for example in C++ or Fortran. A typical analysis performs selections that include computations over input datasets and aggregations over results of the selections. The jobs are submitted to Grid resources and their execution is monitored. In contrast, POQSEC uses a declarative high-level query language to specify analyses and the goal of POQSEC is transparent execution without considering whether the query will be executed on Grid resources or locally.

3 POQSEC Architecture

The architecture presented in Fig. 1 illustrates the current implementation of POQSEC. The POQSEC architecture considers limitations of the NorduGrid (NG) middleware. NorduGrid and its limitations are briefly described in Sect. 3.1. Section 3.2 describes POQSEC components and its interaction with NorduGrid.

3.1 NorduGrid Middleware

NorduGrid (also called Advance Resource Connector) [4,16] is a middleware between Grid users and computational resources that are managed by local batch systems. Thus NorduGrid does not control computational resources; instead it submits user tasks to local batch systems on clusters and each local batch system allocates cluster nodes according to its policy and current load of the cluster.

The *Computing Elements* (CE) are clusters where Grid jobs are executed while *Storage Elements* (SE) are file servers where the data to be queried are stored. The CEs and SEs are managed by NorduGrid and are accessible by submitting Grid jobs to an *NG Client*. The NG client is a set of command line tools to submit, monitor, and manage jobs on the Grid. It also has commands to move data between storage elements and clients, and to query Grid resource information such as loads on different CEs and job statistics. Users of NorduGrid always first initiate communication with the NG client.

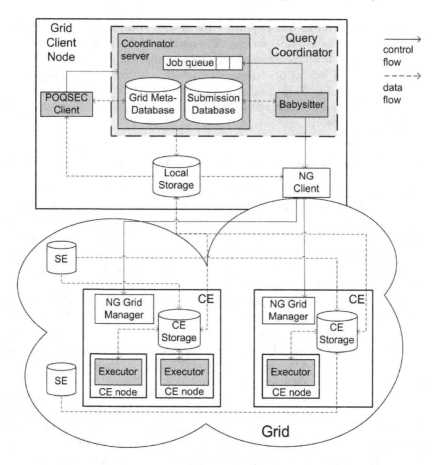

Fig. 1. Architecture of current implementation of POQSEC

The NG client includes a resource brokering service [17] to find suitable resources for jobs. Jobs are described in a resource specification language, *xRSL* [18], which includes specification of, e.g.:

- A user executable and its arguments to be run on some suitable computing element.
- Files to be transported to and from the chosen computing element before and after the execution.
- Maximal CPU time for the execution.
- *Runtime environments* for the execution. A runtime environment is an additional software package required, e.g. an application library such as ROOT [8].
- Standard input, output, and error files for the execution.
- Optional names of the computing elements where the executable can run.
- The number of parallel sub-jobs to be run on the computing element.

In summary NorduGrid requires a lot of user specifications to fully describe computation tasks as xRSL scripts. An example of the script is shown in Fig. 4. POQSEC simplifies this considerably by automatically generating NorduGrid interactions and job scripts to execute a task specified as a declarative query of contents of data. To manage jobs generated by POQSEC, to track their executions, and to download results we provide a *babysitter* integrated with the POQSEC framework.

3.2   POQSEC Components and Their Interaction with NorduGrid

The *Query Coordinator* of POQSEC (Fig. 1) manages user queries submitted to POQSEC for execution on the Grid. It communicates with an NG client directly through a command line interface. Both the query coordinator and the NG client are running on the same node, the *Grid Client Node*, which is a user accessible computer node. On it the user must first initialize his/her Grid credentials required for using NG client services according to the *Grid Secure Infrastructure* (GSI) [19] mechanism.

The *POQSEC Client* component is a personal POQSEC database running on the Grid client node and communicating with the query coordinator. It could also run on a separate node from the Grid client node, e.g. on a user's desktop computer, if GSI is used for the communication with the query coordinator. Queries are submitted through the POQSEC client to the query coordinator for further execution on Grid resources.

The components of the query coordinator are the *Coordinator Server* and the *Babysitter*. The coordinator server contains a *Grid Meta-Database*, a *Submission Database*, and a *Job Queue*. The Grid meta-database stores information about data files and computational elements accessible trough POQSEC. It is needed since Grid resources are heterogeneous and require Grid users to know the computational elements that are able to execute their jobs and properties of the computational elements required for job executions, e.g. runtime environments. POQSEC users need not specify this information when submitting queries since it is stored in the Grid meta-database.

The submission database contains descriptions of queries submitted from the POQSEC client and job descriptions generated by POQSEC to execute the queries. The job queue contains jobs that are created but not yet submitted to NorduGrid for execution.

The process of submitting and evaluating a query is presented in Fig. 2. When a query is received (1) from the POQSEC client the coordinator server first registers the query in the submission database and stores there a number of job descriptions to parallelize the query execution. The number of jobs to create is currently provided by the user as part of the query submission[1]. Information about computational resources and data files from the Grid meta-database is used to generate these job descriptions. xRSL scripts are generated from the job descriptions and are stored (2) in the local storage. Then the jobs are registered

---

[1] We are working on automating this.

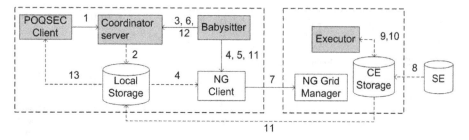

Fig. 2. Interactions between POQSEC components and NorduGrid

in the job queue. The babysitter picks (3) jobs from the job queue and submits (4) them as xRSL scripts to the NG client for execution on Grid resources. Once a job has been submitted the babysitter regularly polls (5) the NG client for its job status and reports (6) the status to the coordinator server to update the submission database. When a job is finished the babysitter downloads (11) the result to the *Local Storage*, which is the file system of the Grid client node, and notifies (12) the coordinator server. The result can be retrieved (13) to the POQSEC client after the query is finished.

On each CE NorduGrid maintains an *NG Grid Manager*. It receives (7) job descriptions from NG clients. In our case these jobs are executing POQSEC subqueries. The NG Grid manager uploads (8) input files from SEs to the local *CE Storage* before each job is submitted to the local batch system. The local batch system allocates *CE nodes* for each job according its policies and current load, and then starts the job executions. For POQSEC these jobs contain *Executors* that evaluate (9) subqueries over uploaded data and store (10) the results in local CE storage files. The babysitter polls (5) the NG client regularly for finished executions. After a job has finished the babysitter requests (11) the NG client to download (11) the result to the local storage of the Grid client node and notifies (12) the coordinator server that the job is ready. Since a given POQSEC query often generates many jobs a query is ready only when all its jobs are finished. However, partial results can be obtained once some jobs are finished.

4   User Application

Our current test application is an application for analyzing data produced by LHC projects for containing charged Higgs bosons [20].

Input data for the analyses are *events*, which describe collision events between elementary particles. Each event comprises sets of particles of various types such as *electrons*, *muons*, sets of other particles called *jets*, and sets of event parameters such as missing momentum in x and y directions (*PxMiss* and *PyMiss*). Each particle is described by its own set of parameters, e.g., the ID-number of the type of a particle (*Kf*), momentum in x, y, and z directions (*Px, Py*, and *Pz*), and amount of energy (*Ee*). The data are stored in files managed by an object-oriented data analysis framework, *ROOT* [8].

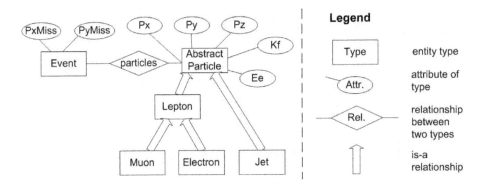

Fig. 3. The schema of the application data

Analysis of events consists of selecting those events that can potentially contain the charged Higgs bosons. A number of predicates, called *cuts*, are applied to each event and if the event satisfies all of them it is selected. A cut is a selection of events of interest for further analysis according to a scientist's theory.

The application is implemented as an extension of a functional and object-oriented mediator system Amos II [21]. It is called *ALEH* (Analysis LHC Events for containing charged Higgs bosons). ALEH has a ROOT wrapper to access data from files managed by ROOT. An object-relational schema of the event data is defined in Fig. 3. It is a view of relevant parts of ROOT files.

A number of analysis queries implementing cuts are defined as *derived functions* expressed in a query language, *AmosQL* [22]. Often a researcher selects events satisfying several cuts. For example, such query in AmosQL is:

```
SELECT ev
FROM Event ev
WHERE jetvetocut(ev) AND zvetocut(ev) AND
    topcut(ev) AND misseecuts(ev) AND
    leptoncuts(ev) AND threeleptoncut(ev);
```

The query is expressed in terms of derived functions, which define the cuts. The definition of one of the cuts in AmosQL is:

```
CREATE FUNCTION zvetocut (Event ev) -> Event AS
SELECT ev
WHERE NOTANY(oppositeleptons(ev)) OR
    (abs(invMass(oppositeLeptons(ev)) - zMass) >= minZMass)
```

where `invMass` calculates the invariant mass of a pair of two given leptons, `zMass` is the mass of a Z particle, `minZMass` is range of closeness, and `oppositeLeptons` is a derived function defined as another query:

```
CREATE FUNCTION oppositeLeptons (Event ev) -> <Lepton, Lepton> AS
SELECT l1, l2
FROM Lepton l1, Lepton l2
```

```
WHERE 11 = particles(ev) AND 12 = particles(ev) AND
      Kf(11) = -Kf(12);
```

5 Implementation

A POQSEC client running our test application ALEH has an interface to a coordinator server through which a user can submit queries for execution in the Grid. It can monitor the status of submitted queries, and can retrieve results of finished queries. To submit a query the user invokes a system interface function named **submit** and specifies there the query defined in terms of the application schema, set of file names which should be processed by the query, number of jobs for parallelization the query, CPU time required for processing one job, and optionally a computing element where the query's jobs should be executed. If no computing element is specified the jobs will be submitted to an NG client along with a list of possible computing elements for execution. The result of the submit function is an object used to monitor the status and to retrieve the result.

The test data, which are events, are produced by ATLAS simulation software and stored on storage recourses accessible through NorduGrid. Paths to the data files are stored in the Grid meta-database of the coordinator server in a format according to xRSL specification [18]. Thus the user provides file names without paths during submission.

For example, the user wants to execute the general analyzing query presented in Sect. 4 over eight specific files containing equal number of events, with parallelization in four jobs that each job will process two files, where the CPU time of executing the query over the two files is 20 minutes, on any of available computational resources of Swegrid. The user submits the query and assigns the result of the submission to a variable :s:

```
SET :s = submit("SELECT ev FROM Event ev WHERE jetvetocut(ev) AND
zvetocut(ev) AND topcut(ev) AND misseecuts(ev) AND leptoncuts(ev)
AND threeleptoncut(ev)",{"bkg2Events_ruslan_000.root",
"bkg2Events_ruslan_001.root","bkg2Events_ruslan_002.root",
"bkg2Events_ruslan_003.root","bkg2Events_ruslan_004.root",
"bkg2Events_ruslan_005.root","bkg2Events_ruslan_006.root",
"bkg2Events_ruslan_007.root"},4,20);
```

The submission is then translated into four xRSL scripts, which are submitted to a NG client for execution. One of the scripts is presented in Fig. 4. The executable there is the ALEH application, which contains the wrapper of ROOT files.

It is necessary for the user to specify which files to analyze to restrict amount of data for processing. In the example the user specifies file names explicitly. Alternatively the user can define a query over the meta-database of the coordinator server to retrieve the file names. The local batch systems of all computational elements available through NorduGrid require specification of CPU time and thus the user needs to provide this[2].

---

[2] We are working to estimate this automatically.

```
& (executable=aleh)
(arguments="aleh.dmp")
(inputfiles= (aleh "/home/udbl/ruslan/Amox/bin/aleh")
  (aleh.dmp "/home/udbl/ruslan/Amox/bin/aleh.dmp")
  (query2005420103329443.osql "query2005420103329443.osql")
  (bkg2Events_ruslan_001.root "gsiftp://se1.hpc2n.umu.se:2811/
se3/ruslan_poqsec/bkg2Events_ruslan_001.root")
  (bkg2Events_ruslan_000.root "gsiftp://se1.hpc2n.umu.se:2811/
se3/ruslan_poqsec/bkg2Events_ruslan_000.root"))
(outputfiles=(result.out ""))
(cputime=20)
(| (runtimeenvironment=ROOT-3.10.02)
  (runtimeenvironment=APPS/HEP/ATLAS-8.0.8)
  (runtimeenvironment=APPS/PHYSICS/HEP/ROOT-3.10.02)
  (runtimeenvironment=ATLAS-8.0.8)
  (runtimeenvironment=APPS/HEP/ATLAS-9.0.3))
(stdin="query2005420103329443.osql")
(stdout="outGen.out")
(stderr="errGen.err")
(gmlog="grid.debug")
(middleware>="nordugrid")
(| (cluster=sg-access.pdc.kth.se) (cluster=bluesmoke.nsc.liu.se)
  (cluster=hagrid.it.uu.se) (cluster=hive.unicc.chalmers.se)
  (cluster=ingrid.hpc2n.umu.se) (cluster=sigrid.lunarc.lu.se))
(jobName="POQSEC: swegrid2005420103329444.xrsl")
```

Fig. 4. Example of the xRSL file with name swegrid2005420103329444.xrsl

The performance of many queries can be significantly improved by parallelization into several jobs. Our experience shows that parallelization of executing a
query gives dramatic improvements. For example, the above submission took 24
minutes. The time was calculated as the elapsed time between when the query was
submitted until all job results were downloaded from the Grid. A submission of the
same query without parallelization as one job took 3 hours and 45 minutes, where
3 hours and 10 minutes were spent for the query evaluation. It is much longer response time compared with the parallelized Grid execution.

During execution of a query submitted to POQSEC the user can monitor its
status by calling status(:s). The status of the query is computed from its batch
jobs statuses. The status "DOWNLOADED" will be returned only if results of all
jobs of the query were downloaded. Then the user can retrieve the result data by
executing retrieve(:s). The result of the query can be retrieved also by using
the function wait(:s). The difference is that if wait is invoked before the result of
the jobs is available the system waits until the coordinator server notifies it that all
jobs are downloaded. Then it retrieves the result while retrieve will just print a
message if the query is not finished[3]. The user can cancel his/her query submission
by executing cancel(:s).

---

[3] We are implementing functions to retrieve partial results.

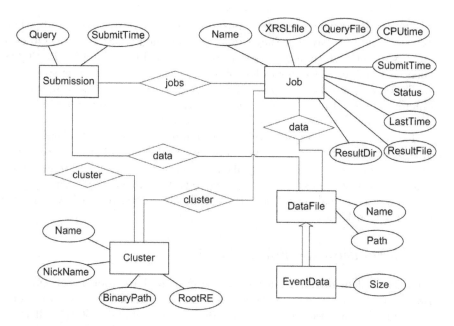

Fig. 5. Schema of the Grid meta-database and the submission database

The coordinator server, the babysitter, and the NG client are running on the same Grid client node as the POQSEC client. The coordinator server contains the Grid meta-database and the submission database. The user is able to query the coordinator server for data from the Grid meta-database and to request updates of the Grid meta-database through the POQSEC client. The babysitter polls the coordinator server to pick up jobs from the job queue and to request updates of the submission database.

A schema of the Grid meta-database and the submission database is presented in Fig. 5. The types Cluster and DataFile and its subtype EventData are parts of the Grid meta-database. The submission database is presented by the types Submission and Job.

When the coordinator server receives query submissions from the POQSEC client it generates job descriptions and creates xRSL files for NorduGrid and script files for POQSEC executors. For example, for the submission given above the coordinator server generates four xRSL files and four script files. Example of one of the xRSL file is given in Fig. 4. The POQSEC script files contain commands for executors to load the input data from the data files through the ROOT wrapper and to execute the user query. In our example one of the script files contains:

```
load_root_file("bkg2Events_ruslan_001.root");
load_root_file("bkg2Events_ruslan_000.root");
save("result.out",SELECT ev FROM Event ev WHERE jetvetocut(ev)
  AND zvetocut(ev) AND topcut(ev) AND misseecuts(ev) AND
  leptoncuts(ev) AND threeleptoncut(ev));
```

The results of the query executions are saved by the executors in files (here in `result.out`) in a way that they can be read by the POQSEC client. Objects, in our case events, which originally were the same, will be treated by the POQSEC client as the same object regardless of that they came from different sources.

The other three xRSL files and three script files are similar except that they have different input data files. Automatic generation of the files by POQSEC exempts the user from manually creating such files for each job.

The main purposes of the babysitter is to interact with the NG client to submit jobs, to monitor status of executing jobs, and to download finished jobs. Each interaction with the NG client can take from several seconds to a minute; thus the coordinator server does not contact the babysitter immediately when a job is created. Instead the babysitter polls the coordinator server regularly when it is not interacting with the NG client.

6   Conclusion and Future Work

We have implemented a framework which provides basic tools for executing long running batch queries on Grid resources over wrapped scientific data distributed in the Grid. The framework is a part of our development of POQSEC (Parallel Object Query System for Expensive Computations), the goal of which is to provide a fully transparent query execution system for scientific applications.

Our on-going work is to automate estimates of maximal CPU time required for the execution of an arbitrary query on a partition of input data. The estimates will be based on probing the query on a number of small samples. We also investigate strategies for suspending those jobs for which the maximal CPU time were underestimated, and then resuming them on other resources.

Another on-going work considers automatic parallelization of a user query submitted for execution on the Grid resources. To decide automatically how many jobs to parallelize the query into depends on the current load of computational resources of the Grid and which computational elements would be chosen for the execution of the generated jobs. We combine this together with development of our own resource brokering algorithm. The resource brokering algorithm will not just decide where to execute the query but also to how many jobs parallelize the query. It should take in account that different computing elements of the Grid have different policies. We will base our resource broker algorithm on job statistics available from the NorduGrid middleware [23].

Job execution on computational resources accessible through NorduGrid can fail and users of NorduGrid need to deal with failures. We are investigating various strategies to deal with failures of job executions.

References

1. ATLAS collaboration. http://atlas.web.cern.ch/Atlas/internal/Welcome.html
2. LHC Computing Grid. http://lcg.web.cern.ch/lcg/
3. EGEE: Enabling Grids for E-sciencE.
   http://egee-intranet.web.cern.ch/egee-intranet/gateway.html

4. Eerola, P., Ekelöf, T., Ellert, M., Hansen, J.R., Konstantinov, A., Kónya, B., Nielsen, J.L., Ould-Saada, F., Smirnova, O., Wäänänen, A.: Science on NorduGrid. In Neittaanmäki, P., Rossi, T., Korotov, S., Oñate, E., Périaux, J., Knörzer, D., eds.: EC-COMAS 2004. (2004) See also http://www.nordugrid.org.
5. LHC - the Large Hadron Collider. http://lhc-new-homepage.web.cern.ch/lhc-new-homepage/
6. Fomkin, R., Risch, T.: Managing long running queries in Grid environment. In Meersman, R., Tari, Z., Corsaro, A., eds.: OTM Workshops. LNCS 3292, Springer (2004) 99–110
7. Swegrid. http://www.swegrid.se
8. Brun, R., Rademakers, F.: ROOT - an object oriented data analysis framework. In: AIHENP'96 Workshop. Nucl. Inst. & Meth. in Phys. Res. A 389 (1997) 81–86 See also http://root.cern.ch.
9. Smith, J., Gounaris, A., Watson, P., Paton, N.W., Fernandes, A.A.A., Sakellariou, R.: Distributed query processing on the Grid. In Parashar, M., ed.: GRID. LNCS 2536, Springer (2002) 279–290
10. Alpdemir, M.N., Mukherjee, A., Gounaris, A., Paton, N.W., Watson, P., Fernandes, A.A.A., Fitzgerald, D.J.: OGSA-DQP: A service for distributed querying on the Grid. In Bertino, E., Christodoulakis, S., Plexousakis, D., Christophides, V., Koubarakis, M., Böhm, K., Ferrari, E., eds.: EDBT. LNCS 2992, Springer (2004) 858–861
11. myGrid. http://www.mygrid.org.uk
12. Narayanan, S., Kurç, T.M., Çatalyürek, Ü.V., Saltz, J.H.: Database support for data-driven scientific applications in the grid. Parallel Processing Letters 13 (2003) 245–271. See also http://storm.bmi.ohio-state.edu.
13. Nieto-Santisteban, M.A., Gray, J., Szalay, A.S., Annis, J., Thakar, A.R., O'Mullane, W.: When database systems meet the Grid. In: CIDR. (2005) 154–161
14. O'Mullane, W., Li, N., Nieto-Santisteban, M.A., Szalay, A.S., Thakar, A.R., Gray, J.: Batch is back: CasJobs, serving multi-TB data on the Web. Technical Report MSR-TR-2005-19, Microsoft Research (2005)
15. Adams, D., Deng, W., Chetan, N., Kannan, C., Sambamurthy, V., Harrison, K., Tan, C., Soroko, A., Liko, D., Orellana, F., Branco, M., Haeberli, C., Albrand, S., Fulachier, J., Lozano, J., Fassi, F., Rybkine, G.: ATLAS distributed analysis. In: CHEP04. (2004)
16. The NorduGrid/ARC User Guide. (2005) Available at http://www.nordugrid.org/documents/userguide.pdf.
17. Ellert, M.: The NorduGrid brokering algorithm (2004) Available at http://www.nordugrid.org/documents/brokering.pdf.
18. Smirnova, O.: Extended Resource Specification Language Reference Manual. (2005) Available at http://www.nordugrid.org/documents/xrsl.pdf.
19. Welch, V., Siebenlist, F., Foster, I., Bresnahan, J., Czajkowski, K., Gawor, J., Kesselman, C., Meder, S., Pearlman, L., Tuecke, S.: Security for Grid services. In: HPDC'03, IEEE Computer Society (2003) 48–57. See also http://www-unix.globus.org/toolkit/docs/3.2/gsi/.
20. Hansen, C., Gollub, N., Assmagan, K., Ekelöf, T.: Discovery potential for a charged Higgs boson decaying in the chargino-neutralino channel of the ATLAS detector at the LHC. SN-ATLAS-2005-050 (2005)
21. Risch, T., Josifovski, V., Katchaounov, T.: Functional data integration in a distributed mediator system. In: The Functional Approach to Data Management: Modeling, Analyzing, and Integrating Heterogeneous Data. SpringerVerlag (2003)

22. Flodin, S., Hansson, M., Josifovski, V., Katchaounov, T., Risch, T., Skold, M.: Amos
    II Release 7 User's Manual. Uppsala Database Laboratory. (2005) Available at
    http://user.it.uu.se/~udbl/amos/doc/amos_users_guide.html.
23. Konstantinov, A.: The Logger Service, Functionality Description and Installation
    Manual. (2005) Available at http://www.nordugrid.org/documents/Logger.pdf.

An Outline of the Global Grid Forum Data Access and Integration Service Specifications

Mario Antonioletti[1], Amy Krause[1], and Norman W. Paton[2]

[1] EPCC, University of Edinburgh, JCMB, The King's Buildings,
Mayfield Road, Edinburgh EH9 3JZ, UK
[2] School of Computer Science, University of Manchester,
Oxford Road, Manchester M13 9PL, UK

Abstract. Grid computing concerns itself with building the infrastructure to facilitate the sharing of computational and data resources to enable collaboration within virtual organisations. The Global Grid Forum (GGF) provides a framework for users, developers and vendors to come together to develop standards to ensure interoperability between middleware from different service providers. Central to this effort is the Open Grid Services Architecture (OGSA), and its associated specifications. These define consistent interfaces, generally couched as web services, and the components required to construct grid infrastructures. Both the web service and grid communities stand to benefit from the provision of consistent and agreed web service interfaces for data resources and the systems that manage them. This paper describes, motivates and presents the context for the work that has been undertaken by the GGF Data Access and Integration Services Working Group (DAIS-WG). The group has defined a set of data access and integration interfaces that are consistent with the OGSA vision. A brief overview of the current family of DAIS specifications is given: WS-DAI specifies a collection of generic data resource properties and messages that are specialised by WS-DAIR and WS-DAIX for use with relational and XML data resources, respectively. The WS-DAI specifications can be applied in regular web services environments or as part of a grid fabric.

Keywords: Data, Databases, Grid, DAIS, OGSA-DAI.

1   Introduction

The *Database Access and Integration Services* Working Group (DAIS-WG) was formed within the *Global Grid Forum* (GGF) to standardise service types and interfaces to allow databases to be seamlessly integrated into grids. From the very beginning the DAIS-WG has aligned itself with the GGF's *Open Grid Services Architecture* (OGSA)[OGSA] vision. The DAIS specifications would then be consistent with and be able to interoperate with the other services and interfaces being proposed for OGSA based grids. The group has in addition been in communication with other standardisation groups, both inside and outside the GGF, to ensure consistency with adjacent standardisation activities. For

J.-M. Pierson (Ed.): VLDB DMG 2005, LNCS 3836, pp. 71–84, 2005.

example, DAIS members are active in the refinement of the GGF OGSA data architecture[1], and outside the GGF, the group has provided use cases for the OASIS *Web Services Resource Framework* (WSRF) technical committee that is producing standards for identifying and interacting with resources in web services. The group has also worked with the Distributed Management Task Force (DMTF) to extend its *Common Information Model* (CIM) with an XML rendering of the CIM model that includes relational metadata.

The primary outcome of the DAIS-WG has been a collection of specifications:

1. *WS-DAI,* which defines properties and message patterns that are independent of the type of data resource that is being accessed [WS-DAI].
2. *WS-DAIR,* which extends WS-DAI with properties and messages for accessing relational data resources [WS-DAIR].
3. *WS-DAIX,* which extends WS-DAI with properties and messages for accessing XML data resources [WS-DAIX].

This paper describes these services, outlining design decisions that have influenced their scope and relationships to existing and emerging standards. The paper is structured as follows. Section 2 describes and motivates the scope of the specifications, and describes how the specifications relate to other web service standards. Section 3 provides an overview of the specifications, which is expanded on in Sections 4. Section 5 describes how the specifications make use of the Web Services Resource Framework, a family of specifications for representing resources in web services. Section 6 presents some conclusions.

2   Scope and Context

In common with most other standardisation activities, the DAIS-WG has iterated towards stable positions on *what* should be included in the standards and *how* these capabilities should be supported. This section reviews several design decisions, with a view to clarifying the role of the DAIS specifications in relation to other web and grid service standards.

2.1   Transparency

Distributed data management is associated with various forms of transparency, which may or may not be supported by an infrastructure. For example, [Ozsu-99] includes the provision of *language, fragmentation* and *replication* transparencies as important functionalities that a data management infrastructure may support. The key design feature behind the DAIS specifications that affects their relationship to such transparencies is that they are designed to provide access to *existing* data management systems. As such, the DAIS specifications are silent with respect to both *fragmentation* and *replication* transparencies; the specifications can be used to access database management systems that support such

---

[1] See http://forge.gridforum.org/projects/ogsa-d-wg for more details.

transparencies or not, but this need not be the concern of the implementer of the specification, and does not surface in the specifications themselves.

A similar position holds with respect to *language* transparency. Many operations in the DAIS specifications take query language statements as parameters. Such operations are generally explicit about the language that is to be used, but DAIS does not require that service implementers parse such language expressions. As such, the DAIS specifications essentially provide web service wrappers for databases; such wrappers will typically pass query language statements directly to an underlying database management system, but are at liberty to intercept, parse, translate or redirect such language statements – DAIS compliant services may implement thin or thick wrappers. As such, the specifications have dependencies on existing query language standards, but are not prescriptive with respect to how a service processes statements provided in such standards.

2.2   Request Composition

Requirements analyses conducted by the DAIS-WG [Atkinson-03] indicated that there was significant demand for services that not only accessed data resources, but which supported flexible data movement and transformation capabilities. For example, there was a widespread need for the ability to express a request that could retrieve data from a database, transform the data using XSLT, and deliver the result to a third party. The DAIS-WG designed simple language interfaces to support such requirements, which formed the basis for the activity model in the widely-used OGSA-DAI system [Antonioletti-05]. However, defining the scope and role of such a language in relation to emerging workflow specifications proved problematic, and the current DAIS specifications support a more limited collection of access patterns that provide extensibility points for more sophisticated data transformation or movement functionalities.

2.3   Metadata

Data access services may have to be able to be discovered and used on the basis of the metadata provided by the services. As such, the DAIS specifications provide a wide range of properties that can be used to describe the behaviour of a service to its consumers. One significant issue for the group has been the provision of an XML Schema for describing the structure of a relational database; such a schema is a complex artifact, which is potentially of use in settings other than DAIS services. As such, the DAIS-WG is working with the Database Working Group of the DMTF to extend the coverage of the CIM database model to include relational metadata from the SQL standard. In parallel with this modelling activity, the DMTF is working to support an XML representation of the complete CIM model, which should be usable by several GGF working groups to describe the properties of resources on a grid.

2.4   Transactions and Security

Web services specifications, such as *web services security* [WS-Security] and *web services atomic transaction* [WS-AtomicTransaction] can be used to specify the security and transaction contexts for a DAIS message. As a result, the DAIS specifications do not provide messages or properties addressing such capabilities. Unfortunately, at the time of writing there are competing proposals for web service transaction standards, and thus the DAIS specifications are likely to complete their standardisation process before there is a widely accepted standard for combining DAIS messages into transactions.

3   Specifications Overview

Before proceeding some DAIS terminology used in the remainder of this paper is outlined. A *data resource* is any entity that can act as a source or sink of data. Data resources may be further sub-classified into: *externally managed data resources* which exist independently of DAIS services and have their lifetime managed by means outside the control of the service, and *service managed data resources* which do not normally exist outside the service-oriented middleware and whose lifetime is controlled by the service. Thus, a database in a DBMS system will normally be in the externally managed data resource category while data stored in memory by a service, which may have been derived from an externally managed data resource, and is accessed via a service will generally be in the service managed data resource category.

A data resource must always have an identifier, an *abstract name*, which is unique and persistent. There is currently an on-going effort to standardise naming of entities within OGSA; for now DAIS uses a URI to represent data resource's abstract names. A DAIS service that provides access to a data resource is called a *data service* – a data service may represent zero or more data resource. The data resource to which a message is targeted at, through a data service, is specified by the provision of the data resource's abstract name in the body of the SOAP message, optionally also including a data resource address in the header of the SOAP message. A *data resource address* is an *End Point Reference* (EPR) as defined in WS-Addressing [WS-Addressing] which also contains the abstract name of the data resource in its *reference parameters*. DAIS mandates the inclusion of the data resource's abstract name in the body of the message so that the messaging framework is the same regardless of whether WSRF is used or not. A *consumer* is an application that exploits a data service to access a data resource.

Two main types of access pattern have been proposed within DAIS. These are represented schematically in Figure 1. *Direct access* mimics the standard request-response pattern currently employed in most web service interactions.

Indirect access uses the factory pattern to create a derived data resource located at the service end. Thus, any data resulting from a consumer-service interaction is not returned to the consumer in the response, as is the case for direct access. Instead, the consumer receives an EPR which can then be used to access the data via a data service. This data service could support a different service interface from the service that created the data resource. This avoids unnecessary data movement and could, in effect, be used as an indirect form of

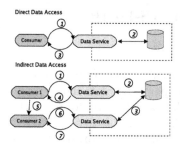

Fig. 1. Direct and Indirect access – the numbering indicates the temporal ordering of the interactions with the corresponding consumers

third party delivery as is illustrated in the picture where the EPR is passed to a second consumer which then pulls the data from the second data service.

The DAIS specifications classifies its interfaces into types originally proposed in the *OGSA Data Services* [OGSA-Data] document:

Data description contains a set of properties – XML elements collected together in a property document – that provide metadata about the underlying data resource and the relationship between the data resource and the data service with which it is associated. Some of these properties are static and are thus informational while others may be changed and may thus affect the behaviour of the service.

Data access collects a set of operations that provide access to a data resource through a data service. These operations implement the direct data access pattern.

Data factory collects together a set of operations that can be used to create derived data resources. These also provide mechanisms to specify the data service interfaces which are to be used to access the data. These operations implement the indirect data access pattern.

Data management was originally also included in this interface classification. However, a management interface could be used to manage: the web service, the data resource through the web service or the relationship between the web service and its associated data resource. The first two types of management were deemed to be out of scope for DAIS as the general management of or through web services is of wider interest than just to the DAIS community. Moreover, the OASIS DMTF TC has provided a set of standards to manage web services and manage entities through web services [MOWS, MUWS]. The DAIS specifications then only provide a limited means for managing the relationship between a data service and its data resource. The next sections consider the specifications in more detail, concentrating on the core messages and properties in the WS-DAI specification together with its WS-DAIR extensions. The principles employed for extending the core interfaces and properties to cater for XML based data resources are very similar and are not covered in this paper – for details see [WS-DAIX].

4   WS-DAI and WS-DAIR

4.1   Message Patterns

The WS-DAI specification defines a set of core properties and operations that are independent of any particular data model used by a data resource. These are then extended by realisations to cater for particular types of data resource. The WS-DAIR and WS-DAIX specifications extend the operations and properties defined in the core document to provide access to XML and relational data resources respectively. The core specifications also provides a set of message patterns that must be observed by realisations. This ensures that DAIS as a whole has a coherent framework. To date most of the effort has been spent in producing realisation for XML and relational data resources although there are preliminary drafts of documents that aim to extend the base DAIS interfaces to deal with object databases and files.

Figure 2 illustrates the message pattern prescribed by the WS-DAI document that is to be used for direct data access interfaces. Note that this is only an illustrative example, for the actual details you should refer to the corresponding specifications. For each of these templates a relational example of its implementation is also shown.

The contents shown in this figure are intended to go in the body of a SOAP message. The **DataResourceAbstractName** identifies the data resource the message is targeting and the **DataFormatURI** specifies the format in which the data should be returned to the consumer. Valid return formats are specified in one or more **DatasetMap** properties set by the service (see later). The query expression is found at the bottom of the message. It is also possible to include parameterised queries with a list of parameters contained in the same request message though this is not shown in this figure. If the query is successful the data is returned to the consumer in the response message. Note that the SQL realisation extends

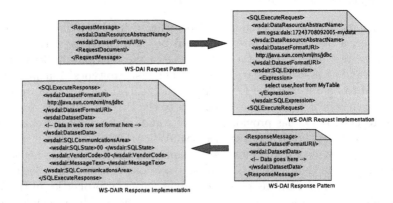

Fig. 2. The DAIS direct data access pattern specified in the core spec and its implementation in the relational specification

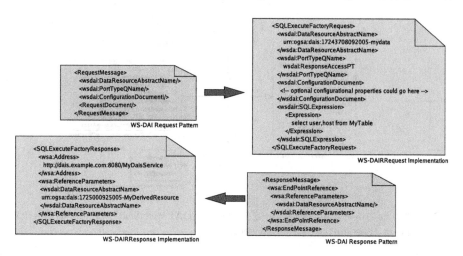

Fig. 3. The DAIS indirect data access pattern specified in the core spec and its implementation in the relational specification

the message pattern to also include information from the SQL communication area.

Figure 3 contains the corresponding message pattern set by the WS-DAI specification for indirect data access together with a WS-DAIR realisation implementation of this pattern.

The request message contains the mandatory data resource abstract name and an optional element containing the QName of the port type with which a data service will provide access to the resulting data. A configuration document allows default values to be set for some of the properties of that data service (values for this are not shown in the figure but the corresponding properties are described in the next Section). The request message contains the query that will populate the resulting data resource. If the query is successful the consumer gets the EPR from which the data may be retrieved.

4.2 Service Properties

Figure 4 shows the properties defined in the WS-DAI specification and the extensions made in the WS-DAIR specification. The different SQL extension groupings reflect the possible service interfaces that can be used to access different types of relational data. The names used for the WS-DAI properties largely describe their purpose. A cursory review is given here but details are left to the WS-DAI specification. Properties can be divided into two general classes: *static properties* which are largely defined by the implementation and cannot be modified and *configurable properties* that may be set by the consumer when they create a data resource using the indirect data access pattern.

The static properties shown in Figure 4: the `DataResourceAbstractName` property provides a place holder for the unique and persistent name of the

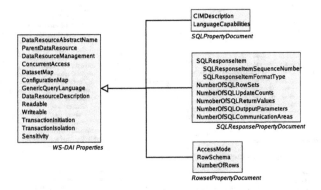

Fig. 4. The core properties defined in the WS-DAI specification and the different extensions to these in the WS-DAIR specification

data resource; the `ParentDataResource` property contains the parent's data resource abstract name if this is a derived data resource otherwise it is empty; the `DataResourceManagement` property indicates whether the data resource is externally or service managed; the `ConcurrentAccess` property is a boolean indicating whether the data service supports concurrent access or not; the `DatasetMap` property provides a means of specifying the valid return formats supported by a data service, there will be one of these elements for each possible supported return type; the `ConfigurationMap` property associates an incoming message type with a valid requested access interface type and a default set of values for the configuration property document; finally the `GenericQueryLanguage` property specifies the valid query languages that can be used with the generic query operation defined in the core spec (see below).

The configurable properties can be set when a new data service-data resource relationship is established: the `DataResourceDescription` allows a human readable description of the data resource to be provided; `Readable` is a boolean indicating whether the data resource can be read by the consumer; the `Writeable` property is another boolean indicating whether the data resource can be written to; the `TransactionInitiation` property enumerates the possible transactional support provided by the service on the arrival of a message – possibilities are: there is no transactional support, an atomic transaction is initiated on the arrival of each message or the message corresponds to a transactional context which is under the control of the consumer; the `TransactionIsolation` property enumerates behaviour of how transactions behave in relation to other on-going transactions, details are left to the specification; finally the `Sensitivity` property describes how sensitive the derived data is to changes in the values of the parent data resource, i.e. whether changes in the parent data resource will be reflected in the derived data or not.

The relational extensions to these base properties are largely self explanatory and are not described here other than for the `CIMDescription` property which is a content holder for an XML rendering of CIM for relational database that is being produced by the DMTF. This will be used by DAIS to provide metadata about the relational data resource. The details of these properties are available in the WS-DAIR specification.

It is perhaps more illustrative to examine the use case represented in Figure 5.

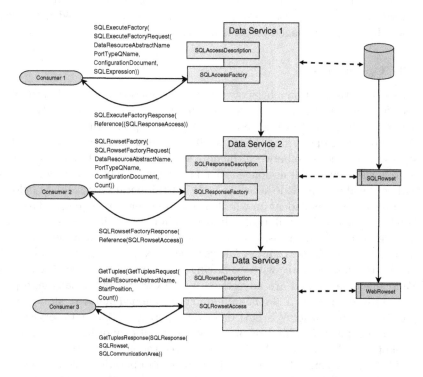

Fig. 5. Example of relational data services

In this example *Data Service 1* is associated with a relational data resource. *Consumer 1* sends a message to the service's `SQLExecuteFactory` operation to create a data resource, populate it with the result set returned from the query sent to the relational data resource and associate this data resource with a data service, *Data Service 2*, that supports an `SQLResponseFactory` interface. The response returned to *Consumer 1* contains the EPR required to access this data. *Consumer 1* passes the EPR to *Consumer 2* which then sends a message to this data service's `SQLResponseFactory` interface to create another data resource which uses a web row set format and is associated with a data service, *Data Service 3*, that supports an `SQLRowsetAccess` interface. *Consumer 2* then gets an EPR which he passes on to *Consumer 3*. *Consumer 3* then finally uses the `SQLRowAccess` to pull the data off the service. This example shows how the different hierarchies of services can be used to access different types of relational data and the context in which the relational property extensions may be used although this has not been shown in this example. Different consumers have been used to indicate the versatility of the pattern though in practise these will generally be the same entity. Clearly it is not necessary to go through all the steps to get a web row set data resource – all that would be required is for *Data Service 1* to support the `SQLResponseFactory` interface for this to happen. Finally, in this instance the first data resource would correspond to an externally managed data resource while the other two derived data resources would be service managed data resources.

4.3   Operations

To conclude this section a brief overview of the operations defined in the WS-DAI specification and the extensions made in the WS-DAIR specification is given. These are illustrated in Figure 6. The WS-DAI specification only defines three core data access operations. There is a `DestroyDataResource` operation that destroys the relationship between the data service and the data resource. Once this is done the service will no longer have any knowledge of that data resource and will not be able to provide access to it. What this entails for the data held in that data resource is dependent on whether it is an externally managed data resource in which case the data will probably remain in place or, if it is a service managed data resource, in which case the data should be removed once the relationship is terminated. The `GenericQuery` allows a query expression to be submitted to the underlying data resource without having to use one of the specialised interfaces. Valid query languages are advertised in the `GenericQueryLanguage` property previously described. A `GetDataResourcePropertyDocument` allows the *whole* property document for WS-DAI defined properties in that data service to be retrieved. Properties within this property document cannot be obtained at a lower level of granularity unless WSRF is used (see the next section).

The `CoreResourceList` is an optional set of operations that may be implemented by a DAIS service. If this is implemented, the list of data resources known to a data service may be retrieved using the `GetResourceList` operation. Also, the EPR corresponding to a data resource's abstract name may be retrieved using the `Resolve` operation.

The relational extensions to the core defined operations have a base `SQLAccess` interface that allows SQL expressions to be submitted to a relational data resource, the results of which will be returned in the response, and an operation to retrieve the `SQLPropertyDocument` which contains metadata about the relational data resource, the data service, and the data service-data resource relationship. A `SQLFactory` interface allows a service managed data resource to be created and populated by the response of a SQL query. The data resource is then associated with an appropriate data service supporting an access interface requested by the consumer. This could use the `ResponseAccess` collection of operations which allow the data to be retrieved as well as finding out about the nature of the response. Likewise, a `ResponseFactory` allows a rowset based data resource to be created that can, in turn, be accessed by using the `RowsetAccess` set of operations. These then are the extensions to the core operations defined in the WS-DAIR specification to cater for relational data resources.

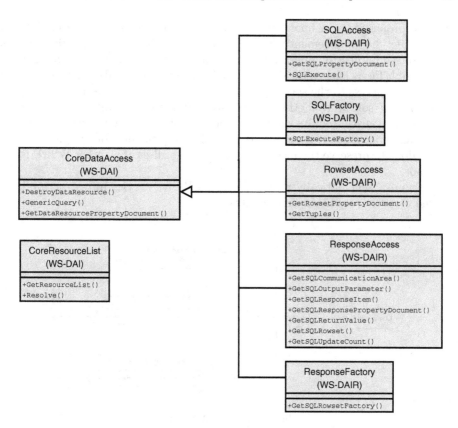

Fig. 6. Operations defined in the WS-DAI specifications and the extensions made in the WS-DAIR specification

Only the core and relational properties and interfaces have been outlined here. The XML extensions follow the same principles and provide support for querying XML data resources using XQuery, XPath, XUpdate as well as operations that manipulate collections and others that provide access to service managed data resources, details are in the WS-DAI specification [WS-DAIX]. It is worth noting that DAIS does not prescribe how these operations are to be combined to form services; the proposed interfaces may be used in isolation or in conjunction with others and, in time, viable compositions of interfaces will follow established patterns for data access.

5   DAIS and WSRF

The core functionality of DAIS has no reliance on WSRF. One can use the base interfaces that have already been outlined in this paper and access the service properties without requiring WSRF, albeit if you do not use WSRF you can only retrieve the whole property document. There are no means provided for getting these properties at a finer level of granularity unless WSRF is used. The soft state lifetime management without WSRF has to be explicit, i.e. the consumer has to send a destroy operation to the data service or the data resource will be accessible for as long as the data service is there. Using WSRF allows one to have fine grain access to the service properties [WS-ResourceProperties] and also use the WSRF soft state lifetime management [WS-ResourceLifetime] but there is a caveat: you still require the data resource abstract name to be included in the message body even if it is only for a WSRF implementation to ignore it. This was done to preserve the message structure regardless of whether WSRF is used or not.

Figure 7 schematically represents how a WSRF service infrastructure is layered over the core DAIS functionality.

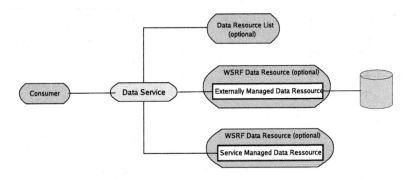

Fig. 7. WSRF DAIS extensions

A data service may represent more than one data resource. If WSRF is used each data resource must have a corresponding WSRF data resource. These are used for both externally and service managed data resources. In order to allow a data resource's abstract name to be mapped to an EPR the optional *data resource list* interface may be implemented which provides such functionality as well as allowing a consumer to obtain a list of all the data resources known to a data service.

This ability to use DAIS without requiring an explicit dependency on WSRF has been undertaken in order to provide a means for those who would like to use DAIS but are not ready to adopt WSRF. The ability to use DAIS without WSRF, in essence, provides a potential upgrade path by allowing service providers to start off with a non-WSRF solution and then, as confidence in WSRF grows, move on to exploit the additional capabilities provided by WSRF.

6   Conclusions

The DAIS specifications only provide web service interfaces to relation and XML data resources. However, the overall framework is extensible, and different groups are exploring the development of additional realisations for object databases, ontologies and files.

The DAIS specifications are intended to provide useful functionalities for describing and accessing data resources, and can be used to support common use cases directly. However, they have really been designed to form part of a wider service-based architecture. As such, standards from the web services community for authentication and transaction management, and from the grid community for data movement and negotiation, can be seen as complementing the DAIS specifications, and facilitating their use in an increasing range of applications.

Acknowledgements. We gratefully acknowledge the input and contributions that have been made to the production of these standards, in particular: Bill Allcock, Malcolm Atkinson, N.Chue Hong, Brian Collins, Patrick Dantressangle, Vijay Dialani, Dieter Gawlick,Shannon Hastings, Allen Luniewski, James Magowan, Sastry Malladi, Inderpal Narang, Savas Parastatidis, Greg Riccardi, Steve Tuecke, Jay Unger, Paul Watson, Martin Westhead, Simon Laws, Susan Malaika, Dave Pearson and the many others who are not explicitly mentioned here.

References

[Antonioletti-05] M. Antonioletti, M.P. Atkinson, R. Baxter, A. Borley, N.P. Chue Hong, B. Collins, N. Hardman, A. Hume, A. Knox, M. Jackson, A. Krause, S. Laws, J. Magowan, N.W. Paton, D. Pearson, T. Sugden, P. Watson, and M. Westhead. The Design and Implementation of Grid Database Services in OGSA-DAI.Concurrency and Computation: Practice and Experience, 2005, Volume 17, Issue 2-4 , Pages 357-376.

[Atkinson-03] M.P. Atkinson, V. Dialani, L. Guy, I. Narang, N.W. Paton, D. Pearson, T. Storey and P. Watson. Grid Database Access and Integration: Requirements and Functionalities. GFD.13. March 13th 2003. http://www.ggf.org/documents/GFD.13.pdf.

[DAIS-Mappings] S. Laws, S. Malladi, S. Parastatidis. Scenarios for Mapping DAIS Concepts. September 1, 2004. http://forge.gridforum.org/projects/dais-wg/document/Scenarios_for_Mapping_DAIS_Concepts/en/3

[MOWS] I. Sedukhin (Ed). Web Services Distributed Management: Management of Web Services (WSDM-MOWS) 1.0. OASIS-Standard, 9 March 2005. http://www.oasis-open.org/apps/org/workgroup/wsdm/download.php/11761/wsdm-mows-1.0.pdf

[MUWS] W. Vambenepe (Ed).Management: Management Using Web Services (MUWS 1.0) Part 1. OASIS Standard, 9 March 2005. http://www.oasis-open.org/apps/org/workgroup/wsdm/download.php/11734/wsdm-muws-part1-1.0.pdf

[OGSA] I. Foster (Ed), H. Kishimoto (Ed), A. Savva (Ed), D. Berry, A. Djaoui, A. Grimshaw, B. Horn, F. Maciel, R. Subramaniam, J. Treadwell, J. Von Reich. The Open Grid Services Architecture, Version 1.0. Global Grid Forum. GFD-I.030. 29 January 2005. http://www.ggf.org/documents/GFD.30.pdf

[OGSA-Data] I. Foster, S. Tuecke, J. Unger, A. Luniewski. OGSA Data Services. February 24, 2004 http://forge.gridforum.org/projects/dais-wg/document/ OGSA_Data_Services-ggf10/en/1

[Ozsu-99] T. Ozsu and P. Valduriez, Principles of Distributed Database Systems, 2nd Edition, Prentice-Hall, 1999.

[WS-Addressing] M. Gudgin (Ed), M. Hadley (Ed). Web Services Addressing 1.0 - Core. W3C Candidate Recommendation 17 August 2005. http://www.w3.org/ TR/ws-addr-core.

[WS-AtomicTransaction] L. F. Cabrera, G. Copeland, M. Max Feingold (Editor) R. W. Freund, T. Freund, J. Johnson, S. Joyce, C. Kaler, J. Klein, D. Langworthy, M. Little, A. Nadalin, E. Newcomer, D. Orchard, I. Robinson, T. Storey, S. Thatte, Web Services Atomic Transaction (WS-AtomicTransaction). Version 1.0. August 2005. ftp://www6.software.ibm.com/software/developer/library /WS-AtomicTransaction.pdf

[WS-DAI] M. Antonioletti, M. Atkinson, S. Malaika, S. Laws, N. W. Paton D. Pearson and G. Riccardi. Web Services Data Access and Integration (WS-DAI). DAIS-WG Specification Version 1.0. Draft, Global Grid Forum. 2005.

[WS-DAIR] M. Antonioletti, B. Collins, A. Krause, S. Malaika, J. Magowan, S. Laws, N. W. Paton. Web Services Data Access and Integration - The Relational Realisation (WS-DAIR) Specification Version 1.0. Draft, Global Grid Forum. 2005.

[WS-DAIX] M. Antonioletti, A. Krause, S. Hastings, S. Langella, S. Malaika, S. Laws, N. W. Paton. Web Service Data Access and Integration - The XML Realisation (WS-DAIX) Specification Version 1.0. Draft. Global Grid Forum. 2005.

[WS-ResourceProperties] S. Graham (Ed), J. Treadwell (Ed). Web Services Resource Properties 1.2 (WS-ResourceProperties), Version 1.2, Committee Draft 01, 19 May 2005. http://docs.oasis-open.org/wsrf/wsrf-ws_resource_properties-1.2-spec-cd-01.pd

[WS-ResourceLifetime] L. Srinivasan (Ed), T. Banks (Ed). Web Services Resource Lifetime 1.2 (WS-ResourceLifetime), Version 1.2, Committee Draft 01, 19 May 2005. http://docs.oasis-open.org/wsrf/wsrf-ws_resource_lifetime-1.2-spec-cd-01.pdf

[WS-Security] Web Services Security v1.0 (WS-Security 2004) [OASIS 200401] http://www.oasis-open.org/committees/ tc_home.php?wg_abbrev=wss

File Caching in Data Intensive Scientific Applications on Data-Grids

Ekow Otoo[1], Doron Rotem[1], Alexandru Romosan[1], and Sridhar Seshadri[2]

[1] Lawrence Berkeley National Laboratory,
University of California, Berkeley, California 94720
[2] Leonard N. Stern School of Business, New York University,
44 W. 4th St., 7-60, New York, 10012-1126

Abstract. We present some theoretical and experimental results of an important caching problem which arises frequently in data intensive scientific applications that are run in data-grids. Such applications often need to process several files simultaneously, i.e., the application runs only if all its needed files are present in some disk cache accessible to the compute resource of the application. The set of files requested by an application, all of which must be in cache for the application to run, is called a *file-bundle*. This requirement introduces the need for cache replacement algorithms that are based on file-bundles rather then individual files. We show that traditional caching algorithms such as *Least Recently Used (LRU)* and *GreedyDual-Size (GDS)* are not optimal in this case since they are not sensitive to file-bundles and may hold in the cache non-relevant combinations of files. We propose and analyze a new cache replacement algorithm specifically adapted to deal with file-bundles. Results of experimental studies of the new algorithm, using a disk cache simulation model under a wide range of conditions such as file request distributions, relative cache size, file size distribution, and incoming job queue size, show significant improvement over traditional caching algorithms such as GDS.

1 Introduction

1.1 Overview

Data intensive scientific applications concern application software that have very large data and storage resource requirements. Such applications are becoming increasingly prevalent in domains of scientific and engineering research. Examples include long running simulations of time-dependent phenomena that periodically generate snapshots of their state as in Astrophysics and climate modeling, simulation of combustion phenomena, and very large data sets generated from experiments such as BaBar [1] or the Large Hadron Collider (LHC) in the domain of high energy particle physics. The large datasets, from simulations and actual experiments, are preprocessed and maintained in units of files on geographically dispersed mass storage systems of a data-grid. Subsequent data analyses and visualization applications retrieve subsets of these files into locally accessible disk storage systems of high performance computing resources. This gives rise to

J.-M. Pierson (Ed.): VLDB DMG 2005, LNCS 3836, pp. 85–99, 2005.

large demands for disk and tape storage resources, and high network bandwidth. The disk storage effectively cache the requested files according to the demands of the application.

Caching has long been recognized as one of the most important techniques for reducing bandwidth consumption [2,3]. The general use of the term caching implies a specialized buffer storage that is used to speed up access when the data is transferred between different levels of a storage hierarchy with different characteristics: speed of access, size and cost per bit (see Fig. 1).

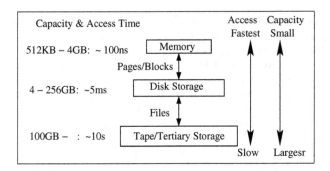

Fig. 1. The Different Levels of Caching in Data Intensive Applications

Successful caching relies on two properties of the access patterns of most application to be effective: *temporal locality* - if a file is accessed once, it is likely to be accessed again soon; *spatial locality* - if a file is accessed then files in close proximity (e.g., on the same storage tape) are also likely to be accessed. In the context of data-grids [4], a middle-ware service such as a storage resource manager [5] or distributed caching service [6], provides staging disks for files being requested. The disk cache manager often has no knowledge of the request stream of files being requested into the cache. Consequently, many cache systems are based on recognition of patterns of either recently used or frequently used files and use this to determine which files should be kept in cache and which should be evicted.

1.2   Problem Description and Previous Work

Consider a sequence of jobs that make requests for files at a computational resource where each job is comprised of one or more file requests. The requests are serviced in some order: *first come first serve (FCFS), shortest job first (SJF),* etc. A cache C of some fixed size $s(C)$, is available for storing a subset of all the requested files. A job is serviced only if all the files it needs are already in the cache C, otherwise it waits in a queue until all its requested files are transferred from a Mass Storage System (located either locally or at a remote site), into C. These data transfers cause time delays for the job execution, as well as consumption of valuable resources such as network and data storage bandwidth.

The problem we address is that of finding an optimal cache replacement policy that maximizes throughput, or alternatively minimizes the volume of data transfered, under a limited cache space. The additional constraint is that all the files in a request must be in the disk cache for the job to run.

We refer to the set of files requested by a job as a *file-bundle*. Processing a job requires that all the files in its *file-bundle* be present simultaneously in the cache. For this reason, it is necessary in this environment to make cache loading and replacement decisions based on *file-bundles* rather then a single file at a time as in traditional file caching algorithms. This difference is quantified further in section 3.

The quest for optimal caching strategies has posed some interesting challenges and has culminated in the development of numerous cache replacement policies some of which include: Least Recently Used (LRU), Least Frequently Used (LFU), Greedy Dual Size (GDS) [7,8] and Minimum Average Cost Per Replacement (MACR). The closest environment, in the use of caching techniques, to the one addressed in scientific data management in data-grids, is that of web-caching where proxy servers and reverse proxy servers are configured essentially as web caches. Other systems that provide similar caching functionalities are the *dCache* [6], and Storage Resource Managers (SRM) [5].

Although the literature provides a considerable number of papers [7,9,8,10] that describe and analyze caching and replacement policies, the main concern of most of these efforts is the maintenance of a "popular" set of files in the cache in order to maximize "hit" ratios and minimize expected access costs for requested files not found in cache. The problem discussed in this paper is radically different from these earlier works as requests require caching of multiple files simultaneously rather than single files.

We propose here algorithms based on an analysis of the problem that maximizes the throughput of jobs, i.e., number of jobs serviced per unit time, while also minimizing the *byte miss ratio* [2,7]. We compare our results with some earlier works on caching, using the *byte miss ratio* as our performance metric for most of the experiments. We also show how the results are affected when queues of waiting jobs are taken into consideration. The rational in choosing *byte miss ratio* (or conversely, the byte hit ratio), metric for comparison is that, we wish to minimize the amount of data transfered into and out of the cache.

1.3   Main Results

The main results of this paper are: i) Identification of a new caching problem, which arises frequently in scientific applications that deal with *file-bundle* caching. ii) Derivation of a new cache replacement algorithm *File Bundle Cache (FBC)*, that is simple to implement. Unlike existing cache replacement algorithms in the literature, we track the *file-bundles* that were requested in the past to determine what combinations of files should be retained or evicted from the cache. This results in a much lower cache miss-ratio under a wide range of conditions tested. iii) Results of extensive simulation runs that compare the *FBC* algorithm with *GreedyDual-Size* [7] cache replacement consistently show that *FBC* gives a much lower average volume of data transfers per request with file requests observing either Uniform or Zipf distributions.

The rest of the paper is organized as follows. In Section 2 we discuss file caching and its significance to data intensive application. In Section 3 we present a heuristic based on a greedy algorithm called *File Bundle Caching (FBC)*. We give a bound from the optimal in this section. This result, using LP relaxation, is derived in [10]. Our experiments carried out to compare our proposed algorithm with GredyDual-Size is introduced in Section 4 and the results are discussed in Section 5. We conclude with Section 6 where we give some directions for future work.

2   File Caching in Scientific Data Management

This work is motivated by file caching problems arising in scientific data management [1,4], and other applications that involve multi-dimensional data [9,11]. One common characteristic of such applications is that they deal with objects that have multiple attributes (10 to 500), and often partition the data such that values for each attribute (or a group of attributes) are stored in a separate file (vertical partitioning). Subsequent analysis and data mining jobs that operate on this data often require that several of these attributes are compared or combined together for further computation. In relational database terminology, this is equivalent to computing a multi-way join.

An example of caching of *file-bundles* comes from the area of bitmap indices for querying high dimensional data [11]. In this case, a collection of N objects (such as physics events) each having multiple attributes, is represented using bitmaps in the following way: the range of values of each attribute is divided into sub-ranges also called bins; a bitmap is constructed for each bin with a '0' or '1' bit indicating whether an attribute value is in the required sub-range. The bitmaps (each consisting of N bits before compression) are stored in multiple files, one file for each bin of an attribute. Range queries are then answered by performing boolean operations among these files. Again, in this case all files containing bitmaps relevant to the query form a *file-bundle* as they must be read simultaneously to answer the query. Other examples of applications that require *file-bundles* are applications that need to compute derived data based on raw data residing in several files. For example applications that analyze physics experimental data coming from detectors, require *file-bundles* consisting of files with measurement data (energy level, momentum etc.) together with other files containing instrument calibration data for proper interpretation of the measurements.

As an example of the type of scientific applications for which our file-bundle caching is relevant, we analyzed trace logs taken from October 1 to October 26, 2004 corresponding to workloads of an actual data intensive scientific applications of the high energy physics BaBar experiment [1]. During this time interval, 504,493 jobs were submitted requesting a total of 2,028,541 files, 86,378 of which were unique. The Figures 2(a) and 2(b) illustrate respectively, the file request

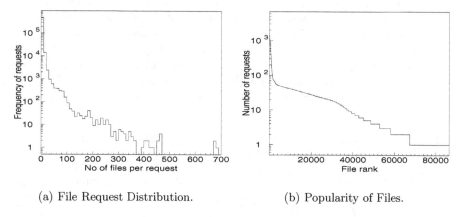

(a) File Request Distribution.   (b) Popularity of Files.

Fig. 2. Sample Workload from BarBar Physics Experiment

distribution and distribution of file occurrences within requests of a sample of the workload from BaBar analysis application.

We note that in this case the size of a file-bundle can vary from 1 to 700 with small sized bundles being the most popular. Also we observe that some files were requested more often, and appeared frequently in most requests, while others were requested only once in the entire workload.

3 Algorithms and Bounds from Optimality

3.1 File Bundle Caching Algorithm

The main idea behind our caching strategy is to load the cache with a set of files that correspond to popular *file-bundles*, thus maximizing the probability that an arriving request can find all its files in the cache. We illustrate the difference between this strategy and caching policies based on single file popularity with a small example. For a given cache state and a request r, we say that the cache supports r or, alternatively, that r is a request-hit if the *file-bundle* needed by r is found in the cache.

Example. Let us assume that we have six possible requests $r_1, r_2, ..., r_6$ each associated with a *file-bundle* drawn from $F = f_1, f_2, ... f_7$ as shown in Table 1. Further, let us assume that all files are of the same size, the cache can hold only three files, and all six requests are equally likely, *i.e.* any request is likely to arrive with a probabilty of $\frac{1}{6}$. Each row in Table 2 shows the probablity of the event that a file is requested by a random request. Note that the sum of probabilities is more than 1 as the events are not mutually exclusive. We note that the most popular file is f_5 as 4 requests out of the six possible requests need it. This is followed by files f_6 and f_7 each needed by 3 of the requests. Each row in Table 3 shows request-hit probablities, *i.e.*, the probablity that a random request will find its *file-bundle* in the cache under some cache content. Only 5 cases of cache content out of the 35 cases (possible ways of choosing 3 files from 7) are shown. We note that keeping the 3 most popular files (row 1 of the Table 3) does not lead to the largest request-hit probability. The best request-hit probability is represented by the second row of Table 3 which has a request-hit probability of $\frac{1}{2}$ since keeping files f_1, f_3, f_5 in the cache results in a request-hit for 3 out of the six possible requests.

Table 1. Requests and their file-bundles

Request	File-Bundle
r_1	f_1, f_3, f_5
r_2	f_2, f_6, f_7
r_3	f_1, f_5
r_4	f_4, f_6, f_7
r_5	f_3, f_5
r_6	f_5, f_6, f_7

Table 2. File request probabilities

File	No of Requests	File req. prob.
f_1	2	1/3
f_2	1	1/6
f_3	2	1/3
f_4	1	1/3
f_5	4	2/3
f_6	3	1/2
f_7	3	1/2

Table 3. Request-hit probabilities

Cache Contents	Requests Supported	Req.-hit prob.
f_5, f_6, f_7	r_6	1/6
f_1, f_3, f_5	r_1, r_3, r_5	1/2
f_1, f_5, f_6	r_3	1/6
f_3, f_5, f_6	r_5	1/6
f_1, f_2, f_3	-	0

We also note that a simplistic approach that loads or evicts *file-bundles* from the cache associated with requests based solely on their popularity (e.g., LFU-Least Frequently Used based algorithms), does not work, since file-sharing between *file-bundles* must also be taken into account. For example, let us consider a small subset of the requests as shown in Fig. 3. The relative popularity of each of the 3 requests is also given. Eviction of the *file-bundle* associated with the relatively unpopular request r_2 (popularity of .2) will cause a cache miss for the highly popular requests r_1 and r_3 (each with popularity of .4) whose *file-bundles* overlap with it. Similar example can be constructed for *file-bundle* LRU based algorithms as well. For that reason, the degree of file-sharing must also be taken into account by an effective cache replacement algorithm. We now proceed to describe our File Bundle Caching *(FBC)*, algorithm, which loads and evicts files from the cache in response to new requests.

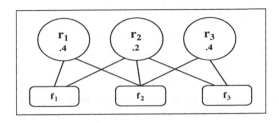

Fig. 3. Example file-bundle overlaps

At the heart of our caching strategy is an algorithm called *OptCacheSelect*, called by *FBC*, to determine which files must be loaded and/or replaced. We will first describe *OptCacheSelect* and then show how it is incorporated into the main algorithm *FBC*. It takes into account file sizes and request frequency counts as well as degree of file-sharing. It will be described in more detail below. The result produced by *OptCacheSelect* is a new set of files loaded into the cache that attempts to maximize request-hit probability. The algorithm is a greedy heuristic that attempts to achieve a good approximation to an NP-hard problem that is a generalization of the Knapsack problem.

The *OptCacheSelect* algorithm takes as its input a data structure $L(R)$ containing full information about a collection of historical requests R. The data structure $L(R)$ is initially empty and gets updated with each request processed. For lack of space we will not present here the exact implementation of $L(R)$, which is basically a hash-table with pointers to other structures, but rather describe its contents. For each request $r_i \in R$ that was served by the system we store in $L(R)$ the following information:

- An associated value $v(r_i)$. In our current implementation $v(r_i)$ is simply a counter incremented by 1 each time the same request appears but, it can also reflect request priority or some other measure of importance. In Section 5 we show how this function can be used to enhance "fair" scheduling of the requests.
- the set $F(r_i)$ of files requested by r_i and the size of each such file.

We need the following additional definitions in the description of the algorithm. We denote the size of a cache C by $s(C)$. For a file f_i, let $s(f_i)$ denote its size and let $d(f_i)$ represent the number of requests served by it. The adjusted size of a file f_i, denoted by $s'(f_i)$, is defined as its size divided by the number of requests it serves, i.e., $s'(f_i) = s(f_i)/d(f_i)$.

The adjusted relative value of a request, or simply its relative value, $v'(r_j)$, is its value divided by the sum of adjusted sizes of the files it requested, *i.e.*

$$v'(r_j) = \frac{v(r_j)}{\sum_{f_i \in F(r_j)} s'(f_i)}$$

The algorithm *OptCacheSelect(L(R),S(C))* attempts to select an optimal set of files that fits in the cache in order to serve a subset of R with the highest total value. It does so by servicing requests in decreasing order of their adjusted relative values skipping requests that cannot be serviced due to insufficient space in the cache for their associated files. The final solution is the maximum between the value of requests loaded and the maximum value of any single request. The justification for the comparison is given in [10]

The intuition behind using $v'(r_j)$ as a measure for ranking requests is that $v'(r_j)$ increases with an increase in request popularity and degree of sharing of its files with other requests. On the other hand, it decreases when the amount of cache resources used by $F(r_j)$ grows.

In practice, we even do better by recomputing $v'(r_j)$ for all requests r_j not selected yet, and resorting the requests in decreasing order of adjusted values,

Input : A data structure $L(R)$ as described above and a cache C of size $s(C)$

Output: The solution G - a subset of the requests in R whose files must be loaded into the cache.

Step 0: /* *Initialize* */
$G \leftarrow \phi$;   //set of requests selected
$s(C') \leftarrow s(C)$;   // $s(C')$ keeps track of unused cache size
Step 1: Sort the requests in R in decreasing order of their relative values and renumber from $r_1, \ldots, r_n$ based on this order
Step 2:
for $i \leftarrow 1$ **to** n **do**
    if $s(C') \geq s(F(r_i))$ **then**
        Load the files in $F(r_i)$ into the cache
        $s(C') \leftarrow s(C') - s(F(r_i))$;   // update unused cache size
        $G \leftarrow G \cup r_i$;   // add request r_i to the solution
    end
end
Step 3: Compare the total value of requests in G and the highest value of any single request and choose the maximum.

Algorithm 1: Algorithm OptCacheSelect

following Step 2. This is done by setting to 0 the size of files in $F(r_j)$ that are already in the cache since these files will not consume any additional cache resources. This leads to an increase in adjusted value for requests that share files with the previously selected requests.

We are now in a position to describe the main steps of our caching algorithm, FBC, as illustrated in Fig. 4. Initially the cache is empty, whenever a new request r_{new} arrives all its missing files (files requested by it but not currently in the cache) are loaded into the cache (Fig. 4a). At some point the cache fills up (Fig. 4b) and a caching replacement decision must be taken when a new request, r_{new}, arrives.

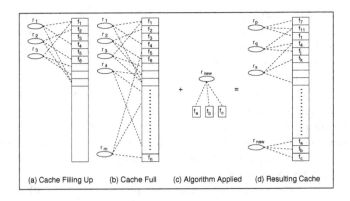

(a) Cache Filling Up   (b) Cache Full   (c) Algorithm Applied   (d) Resulting Cache

Fig. 4. The steps of algorithm FBC

All files requested by r_{new} not currently present in the cache must be loaded into the cache and some other files currently in the cache must be evicted in order to make space for them (Fig. 4c). We compute S, the space requirement for the new files requested by r_{new}, and then call on algorithm *OptCacheSelect* described above to decide on the optimal files that must be maintained in the remaining part of the cache $s(C) - S$, to maximize request-hit probability (Fig. 4d). Algorithm 2 formalizes the steps of the *FBC* algorithm.

Input : A new request r_{new}, a data structure $L(R)$ including
information about requests $R = \{r_1, \ldots r_n\}$, their values
$v(r_j)$, the sets $F(r_i)$, a cache C of size $s(C)$,$F(C)$ the set of
files currently in the cache, and the sizes $s(f_i)$ of all files
requested by members of R.

Output: The solution G - a set of files that must be loaded into C

Step 1: Compute S, the amount of space needed by files in $F(r_{new})$
that are not currently in the cache C

Step 2: Call *OptCacheSelect(L(R),s(C)-S)* and store its solution in
$F(Opt)$

Step 3: Load into the cache C the files in $F(Opt) \backslash F(C)$

Step 4: Update the data structure $L(R)$ with all relevant information
about r_{new}

Algorithm 2: Algorithm OptFileBundle

3.2   Complexity of the Algorithm

An analysis of the algorithm is presented in [10], where we formulate the problem as a lnear programming one and its dual. Due to space limitation, we only state the main results of the analysis in the following theorem.

Theorem 1. *Let $V_{OptCachSelect}$ represent the value produced by Algorithm Opt-CachSelect and let V_{OPT} be the optimal value. Let d^* denote the maximum degree of a file, i.e., $d^* = \max_i d(f_i)$ then*

$$\frac{V_{OPT}}{V_{OptCachSelect}} \leq 2d^*.$$

The proof of the above theorem is given in [10]. In practice the value of d^* is quite small as it represents the maximum number of requests sharing the same file. In extreme cases, if a small number of files have large degrees, we can keep them permanently in the cache, and d^* then represents the maximum degree among the remaining files. Also it is interesting to note that in the purely random case, where each request r_i, picks randomly a set of $k = |F(r_i)|$ out of n files, for $k \ll n$ and $r = O(n)$, the expected value of d^*, $E(d^*)$, satisfies $E(d^*) \sim \frac{\log n}{\log \log n}$ (See [12], pp. 94).

4 Simulation Framework

We designed a simulation model to explore how the *FBC* algorithm compares with the *GreedyDual-Size* algorithm [7,8]. For that purpose, we implemented a modified version of *GreedyDual-Size* where each request is for a set of files rather than a single file as in the original implementation. The modified GDS algorithm is given in Algorithm 3. Each cached file f is associated with a value $H(f)$ defined by the cost $c(f)$ of reading the file into cache, and the size $s(f)$ of the file. Whenever space is required, the file selected for eviction is that with the minimum $H(f)$ value. By maintaining cached files as a *min-heap* data structure based on the $H(f)$ values, the selection of candidates for eviction is done in logarithmic time. The modification of the *GreedyDual-Size* to *GreedyDual-MF* is conducted by repeated eviction of the file q which has the minimum H value until all the files in the new request can be accommodated in the cache.

Input: A request stream $R = r_1, r_2, ...N$, a cache C of size $s(C)$,
$F(C)$, the set of files currently in cache. Note: a request is for a set of files $r_i = \{f_0, f_1, \ldots, f_{r_i}\}$

Result: Loading of the cache that satisfies GreedyDual-Size Algorithm for each request r_i.

Initialize $L \leftarrow 0$;
for $i \leftarrow 1$ *to* N **do**
    Get next request
    Set $req \leftarrow r_i$;
    foreach $f \in req$ **do**
        if *f is already in cache C* **then**
            $H(f) \leftarrow L + c(f)/s(f)$;
        else
            while *there is not enough room in C to hold f* **do**
                Set $L \leftarrow \min_{\substack{q \in C \\ q \notin r_i}} H(q)$;
                Evict q such that $H(q) = L$;
                Load f into the cache C ;
                Set $H(f) \leftarrow L + c(f)/s(f)$;
            end
        end
    end
end

Algorithm 3: Algorithm GDS-MF

4.1 Workload Characterization

We constructed a simulated workload consisting of a given set of jobs, with each job requesting a random number of files from a pool of available files. The parameters chosen for our simulated workload are as close as possible to observed real experiments that log single file requests at a time. The size of each file was generated randomly between a minimum size of 10 MB and a maximum size of 300 MB. The set of files requested by each job was chosen uniformly from the list of available files such that the total size of the files requested by any given job was smaller than the available cache size. The cache sized varied between 5 GB and 100 GB. Each simulation run consists of generating a large number of jobs ($\approx$ 20000) and selecting a number of them (typically 10000) using either a uniform or Zipf distribution to study the effects of the various parameters.

4.2   Simulation Environment

The simulation program, *cacheSim*, was written in *C++* with extensive use of STL. Using a cluster of three 1.6 GHz dual Opterons with 2GB of RAM each, we ran a large number of experiments to study the behaviour of the proposed algorithms for different combinations of parameters. These experiments consumed over 1000 hours of CPU time. The main performance metric used is the *byte miss ratio* and this was observed primarily for two different workload distributions, and varying cache sizes. There are several parameters of interest that affect the result of the simulation:

Popularity Distribution. The popularity distribution of requests for typical workloads is very hard to characterize as it varies widely from setup to setup and even from day to day. As such we are looking at the effects of the two extremes: a purely random distribution, and a Zipf one.

Cache Size. Given requests of a known average size, varying the cache size determines the number of requests that can fit in cache at any given time. The more requests already in cache, the more likely that files requested by an incoming job are already present in cache.

Incoming Queue Length. Instead of processing a job as soon as it is submitted, one can also consider aggregating the jobs in an incoming queue of a given length, and only submitting the best job once the queue is full.

Queueing Fairness. Requests with a consistently low value stay queued for a large number of iterations. To improve the fairness of the queueing algorithm, we increase the value of a request in queue by a function of the number of iterations the request has been waiting.

5   Discussion of Results

In this section we present results of our simulation runs where we studied the effects of various caching parameters on the performance of our algorithm. The first set of experiments performed involved job popularity distributions. A uniform popularity distribution means that every request from the pool of available requests is equally likely to be requested, whereas Zipf's distribution assigns a probability of selection proportional to $\frac{1}{i}$ to the ith most popular request.

Figures 5(a) and 5(b) compare the *byte miss ratio* for uniform and Zipf request distributions. The cache replacement strategy based on the *FBC* algorithm is superior to the one based on the *GDS* algorithm in the sense that the byte miss ratio is lower. The improved performance of the *FBC* algorithm is attributed to keeping requests coherent in the cache, as well as keeping track of the popularity of each request. The latter is evident when we consider a Zipf distribution where a small set of requests occurs with a high frequency. The *FBC* algorithm increases the value of each request by keeping track of its popularity thus increasing the likelihood of the request staying in the cache.

The overall effect of varying the cache size on the byte miss ratio is shown in Figure 6, where the *Relative Cache Size* is defined to be the ratio of the total size of the files requested to the cache size. As the cache is able to serve more requests the amount of data moving into the cache for each request decreases. Three factors contribute to this effect: 1) the number of files common to all the requests already cached increases, thus minimizing the amount of new data that needs to be brought into the cache, 2) the likelihood of often seen requests to be already in the cache increases, and 3) the efficiency of the *FBC* algorithm improves with the number of requests considered when making a decision as to what requests to keep in cache. The first factor dominates the improved byte miss ratio for the uniform distribution shown in Fig. 6(a) while the second one dominates for the Zipf distribution in Fig. 6(b), hence the dramatic improvement in performance with increasing the cache size.

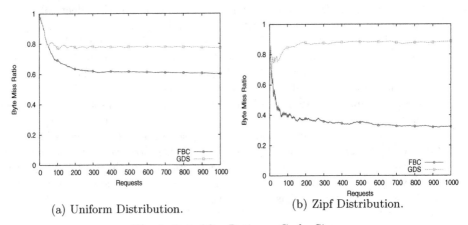

(a) Uniform Distribution.   (b) Zipf Distribution.

Fig. 5. Byte Miss-Ratio vs. Cache Size

Another set of experiments performed involved aggregating the jobs in a processing queue of varying length instead of processing them in FIFO order. Once the queue is full, we run the *FBC* algorithm on the queued requests, and then process the request with the highest value. We do not discuss the details of the results due to lack of space. However, a negative consequence of queuing requests is that requests with a consistently low value may experience starvation, i.e., stay queued for a large number of iterations. Figures 7(a) and 7(b) show the queueing effects for uniform and Zipf distributions, respectively, for a queue

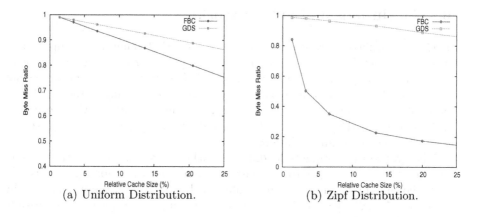

Fig. 6. Effect of Varying Cache Size

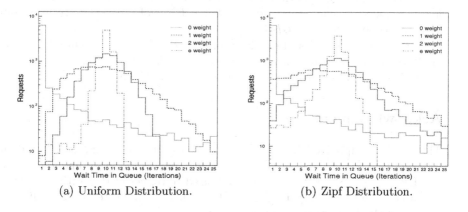

Fig. 7. Queue Wait Time (in iterations) for different "anti-starvation" functions - Log Plot

length of 10: while the majority of requests are scheduled right away, there exists a tail of requests which linger in the queue for a large number of iterations. To mitigate the situation we artificially increase the value of a request in queue by an "anti-starvation" function that takes into account the number of iterations i the request has been waiting in the queue before being scheduled for execution. Three different functions were considered: increase the request value by 1) i (*1-weight*), 2) i^2 (*2-weight*), and 3) 2^i (*e-weight*). Since the value of a request depends on its popularity, the effect of increasing a request value by *1-weight* or *2-weight* on the wait time is less pronounced for a Zipf distribution than for a uniform one since the natural increase in value with popularity of the most often requested requests is of about the same order of magnitude. Only when we artificially increase the value of a queued request by *e-weight* for a Zipf distribution we begin to see it dominate the natural increase with popularity.

6   Conclusions and Future Work

We have identified a new type of caching problem that is notable in applications where multiple files must be in cache for an application to access them concurrently. This problem arises in various scientific and commercial applications but in the use of storage resource manager to service file staging in the problem is particularly significant. Traditional cache replacement policies, where decisions as to which files should be cached or evicted, are based on one file request at a time, fail to give optimal solutions.

The problem of optimally loading the cache so as to maximize the value of satisfied requests is NP hard. We have proposed approximation algorithms that were shown analytically to produce solutions bounded from the optimal one by a factor of $1/(2d^*)$. Extensive simulations that compare our proposed algorithm, FBC with a variant of the GreedyDual-Size (GDS), that handles multiple file requests at a time, show that the proposed algorithms outperform the GDS for both uniform and Zipf distributions. The difference in Zipf distribution was even more pronounced. The results indicate that FBC involves less data transfers into and out of the cache than GDS.

Our future work will address incorporating the FBC algorithm in an actual application environment, such as the data-grid, where large scale data intensive scientific applications are being scheduled to run in the future.

Acknowledgment

This work is supported by the Director, Office of Laboratory Policy and Infrastructure Management of the U. S. Department of Energy under Contract No. DE-AC03-76SF00098. This research used resources of the National Energy Research Scientific Computing (NERSC), which is supported by the Office of Science of the U.S. Department of Energy.

References

1. BaBar: (The babar collaboration http://www.slac.stanford.edu/bfroot/)
2. Andrade, H., Kurc, T., Sussman, A., Borovikov, E., Saltz, J.: On cache replacement policies for servicing mixed data intensive query workloads. In: Proc. 2nd Workshop on Caching, Coherence, and Consistency, with the 16th ACM Int'l. Conf. on Supercomputing, New York, NY (2002)
3. Reiner, B., Hahn, K.: Optimized management of large-scale datasets stored on tertiary storage systems. IEEE Distributed Systems Online Magazine (2004)
4. Chervenak, A., Foster, I., Kesselman, C., Salisbury, C., Tuecke, S.: The Data Grid: Towards an architecture for the distributed management and analysis of large scientific datasets. J. Network and Computer Applications **23** (2000) 187 – 200
5. Shoshani, A., Sim, A., Bernardo, L.M., Nordberg, H.: Coordinating simultaneous caching of file bundles from tertiary storage. In: Proc. 12th Int'l. Conf. on Scientific and Stat. Database Management, SSDBM'2000. (2000) 196 – 206

6. Ernst, M., Fuhrmann, P., Gasthuber, M., Mkrtchyan, T., Waldman, C.: dCache: a distributed data caching system. In: Computing In High Energy And Nuclear Physics, CHEP'01. (2001)
7. Cao, P., Irani, S.: Cost-aware WWW proxy caching algorithms. In: USENIX Symposium on Internet Technologies and Systems. (1997)
8. Young, N.: On-line file caching. In: SODA: ACM-SIAM Symposium on Discrete Algorithms (A Conference on Theoretical and Experimental Analysis of Discrete Algorithms). (1998)
9. Otoo, E.J., Rotem, D., Shoshani, A.: Impact of admission and cache replacement policies on response times of jobs on data grids. In: Int'l. Workshop on Challenges of Large Applications in Distrib. Environments, Seatle, Washington, IEEE Computer Society, Los Alamitos, California (2003)
10. Otoo, E.J., Rotem, D., Romoson, A., Seshadri, S.: File caching in data intensive scientific applications. Technical report, Lawrence Berkeley National Laboratory, LBNL Report No 55587 (2004)
11. Wu, K., Koegler, W.S., Chen, J., Shoshani, A.: Using bitmap index for interactive exploration of large datasets. In: SSDBM'2003, Cambridge, Mass. (2003) 65–74
12. Devroye, L.: Lecture notes on bucket hashing. Birkhauser, Boston (1985)

RRS: Replica Registration Service for Data Grids

Arie Shoshani, Alex Sim, and Kurt Stockinger

Computational Research Division,
Lawrence Berkeley National Laboratory,
University of California,
1 Cyclotron Road, Berkeley, California 94720, USA
{AShoshani, ASim, KStockinger}@lbl.gov

Abstract. Over the last few years various scientific experiments and Grid projects have developed different catalogs for keeping track of their data files. Some projects use specialized file catalogs, others use distributed replica catalogs to reference files at different locations. Due to this diversity of catalogs, it is very hard to manage files across Grid projects, or to replace one catalog with another.

In this paper we introduce a new Grid service called the Replica Registration Service (RRS). It can be thought of as an abstraction of the concepts for registering files and their replicas. In addition to traditional single file registration operations, the RRS supports collective file registration requests and keeps persistent registration queues. This approach is of particular importance for large-scale usage where thousands of files are copied and registered. Moreover, the RRS supports a set of error directives that are triggered in case of registration failures. Our goal is to provide a single uniform interface for various file catalogs to support the registration of files across multiple Grid projects, and to make Grid clients oblivious to the specific catalog used.

1 Introduction

Managing a large number of files at distributed locations is one of the challenges that many large-scale scientific experiments face. For efficiency reasons, many of the files are replicated in multiple storage systems. In order to keep track of the files and their replicas, various file and replica catalogs are used. Typical questions are: What is the name-space for files registered in the catalogs? Shall the catalog be organized as a centralized or decentralized service? How can information about files be retrieved efficiently? How can different sites interact with each other's catalogs? In order to solve some of these issues, various Grid projects have developed different catalogs for keeping track of their data files. Some experiments use specialized file catalogs, others use distributed replica catalogs to reference files at different locations. This diversity of catalogs makes it very hard to manage files across Grid projects or even within a single project. The solution to this problem is not to attempt and standardize a particular file catalog

J.-M. Pierson (Ed.): VLDB DMG 2005, LNCS 3836, pp. 100–112, 2005.

system. Rather, the approach taken here is to provide a uniform specification of a functional interface that permits the multiplicity of catalogs to co-exist. This approach is similar to many commercial products (such as relational database systems) that have a common functional interface specification that permits multiple systems to co-exist. Furthermore, our approach isolates the Grid client programs from the specific catalog system used.

In this paper we introduce a Grid service called the Replica Registration Service (RRS), that provides a uniform functional interface to various file catalogs, replica catalogs, and meta data catalogs. It can be thought of as an abstraction of the concepts used in catalog systems to register files and their replicas. Some experiments may prefer to support their own file catalogs (which may have their own specialized structures, semantics, and implementations) rather than use a standard replica catalog. Providing a RRS that can interact with such a catalog can permit that catalog to be invoked as a service in the same way that other more general-purpose replica catalogs do. If at a later time the experiment wishes to change to another file catalog, it is only a matter of developing a RRS for that new catalog and replacing the existing catalog. Similarly, an existing replica location service (RLS, [3]) that supports the RRS interface can be plugged in instead of the current catalog. In addition, some systems use meta-data catalogs or other catalogs to manage the file name-spaces, and those could be accessed through the same RRS interface as well.

The main contributions of this paper are as follows:

- We introduce a novel Grid service - the Replica Registration Service. We discuss the design considerations and the main functional interface components.
- We report on our experience of using an early implementation of a RRS in a production environment. The results show that the RRS could greatly simplify the management of replicas and reduce registration errors.

2   Related Work

An early version of a replica management framework is presented in [4] where the terms *Replica Management* and *Replica Selection* are defined within the context of a Data Grid. In the European Data Grid Project a similar replica management framework was implemented [7]. An integrated approach for data and meta-data management is provided in the Storage Resource Broker (SRB) [1]. In general, data replication can be done at the file or object level, where multiple objects can either be stored in a single file, or a single object can be stored across multiple files. The differences between object and file replication are discussed in [13]. However, in practice only file replicas are cataloged so far, since the number of objects can be much larger than the number of files. Moreover, the implementation of object replication systems is more complex. For this reason, we focus on file replica registration only in this paper.

In the early days of Grid computing, replicas were stored in LDAP catalogs. Due to performance issues, subsequent replica catalogs or replica location services stored the replicas in relational databases [3]. In recent projects, various file and replica catalogs were implemented for different experiments that are often not compatible [2,6].

Currently, different organizations that use the Grid, develop their own specialized version of replica catalogs. They vary in their functionality greatly. For example, some support GUIDs and LFNs, some support only a single LFN; some support logical and physical directories and some only a single level; some include extensive meta-data information, such as file usage and some have no meta-data at all. Our purpose in this paper is to identify a reasonable set of replica registration functionality independent of any specific implementation. We hope that this approach will provide a uniform interface that will allow for multiple implementations to co-exist.

3   Terminology and Name-Space

3.1   GUIDs, LFNs, and PFNs

There are several ways to refer to a file. If the location of the file is known, one can specify its Physical File Name (PFN). However, since a file may have multiple replicas, it is convenient to refer to the file by using Logical File Names (LFN). Some communities of users prefer to support a unique immutable LFN for each file, and provide a mapping between the LFN and one or more Physical File Names (PFNs). In many cases, LFNs are designed to be structured names. This is a desired property, since the file name conveys a meaning, such as the date, purpose, or conditions that were used at the time the file was generated. However, having such structured names makes it difficult to guarantee global uniqueness of the name. Furthermore, there may be a need to change file names over time, or even have multiple aliases for a file name. For this reason, some communities use a *globally unique identifier*, referred to as GUID, to identify a file, in addition to a LFN. Given that a GUID is used for a file, that file can now have multiple LFNs that are treated as name-aliases for the GUID.

Since we wish to have this specification applicable to all communities, we adopt the more general case of having a GUID for a file. In addition, we permit multiple LFNs per GUID. For communities that only use a single LFN and no GUID, we consider that LFN to be equivalent to a GUID.

The one-to-many relationships between a GUID-to-PFNs and a GUID-to-LFNs are shown schematically in Figure 1. Note that we use SURL (Site URLs) as a generalization of PFNs. The reasons for that are explained next in Section 3.2.

3.2   SURLs as a Generalization of PFNs

Specifying a Physical File Name (PFN) is straightforward. It is specified as a URL made of the format: protocol://machine:port/directory-path/file-name. For example: gridftp://cs.berkeley.edu/home/data. Note that the protocol specified in this case is the transfer protocol.

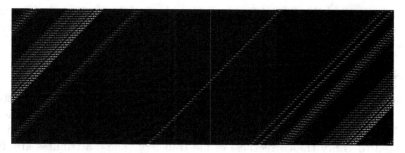

Fig. 1. The relationships between SURLs, GUIDs, and LFNs

Some storage systems support multiple physical devices and multiple directories, and may want to have the freedom of changing the physical location of a file without changing the reference to it by Grid clients. An example of a software layer that permits this functionality is a Storage Resource Manager (SRM) [9]. The SRM is a single endpoint for accessing a file regardless of its physical location on a particular site. The site is a virtual entity referring to the collection of resources under the administrative control of the site manager. The concept of a site permits a single filename to be assigned to a physical file regardless of it physical storage location.

The reference for a file on a site is called a *Site URL* (SURL). For example: srm://data.berkeley.edu:4004/dir/data is the name of a file managed by a SRM residing on the machine data.berkeley.edu, on port 4004. When requesting the file from the SRM using the SURL, the SRM returns the *transfer URL* (TURL) which is the actual PFN. For example, for the file above the SRM may return the PFN on another machine, cs.berkeley.edu, by using the URL gridftp://cs.berkeley.edu/home/data. Note that a PFN is a special case of an SURL, where the transfer service specified by the protocol is the site endpoint. Therefore, we only use SURL in the remainder of this document.

3.3 The LFN Name-Space Structure

LFNs are commonly organized into directory structures, similar to any file system (such as the Unix file system). Some file systems consider directory names as LFNs as well and assign GUIDs to them (this can be automatically assigned by the catalog). The value of treating directories as LFNs is that one can refer to a directory path in a similar way as a reference to a file. In this specification we allow the creation and removal of directories and references to them, so that systems that support this feature will be accessible through the RRS. This is shown schematically in the box referring to LFNs in Figure 1 by having the directory icon in it.

A common use case for using multiple LFNs is that a file is first registered with a particular LFN, and then additional LFNs are allowed to refer to the same file. The original registration is sometimes referred to as the *primary LFN*, and subsequent references to it are referred to as *secondary LFNs* or as *LFN-aliases*.

We do not find this distinction generalizable, useful, or necessary. Therefore we refer to all LFNs in the same way regardless of when they were defined. Thus, the RRS interface does not permit references to *primary LFNs*, only to LFNs.

3.4 File Attributes

File attributes are associated with GUIDs as shown in Figure 1. These attributes represent only global properties that do not depend on where the file resides (the SURL site) and how it is named (its LFNs). Some attributes are considered essential to verify the correctness of file transfers. These attributes are: fileSize, checkSumType, and checkSumValue. We refer to these attributes as *core attributes*. In addition, there may be other attributes that the underlying catalogs may store. We permit the entry and retrieval of all such attributes through the RRS interface. When requesting these attributes, one can refer to *core attributes* only, or to "all" attributes. The RRS will return an array of triples: fileAttribute-Name, fileAttributeType, and fileAttributeValue. Note that all values are passed through the interface as strings. The fileAttributeType refers to the type of the attribute, as it is stored in the underlying catalog. The RRS was designed to have functions to retrieve the attribute values.

4   Replica Management Architecture

Before discussing the Replica Registration Service, we provide an outline of the replica management architecture which is based on the following three components: (a) the Replica Selection Service (RSS), (b) the Replica Copying Service (RCS), and (c) the Replica Registration Service (RRS). This is shown in Figure 2.

Given a GUID or a LFN of a file that has to be replicated to a target site, the Replica Management Service (RMS) first invokes the RRS in order to find all possible replicas. It can then choose to ignore some of these replicas based on its own

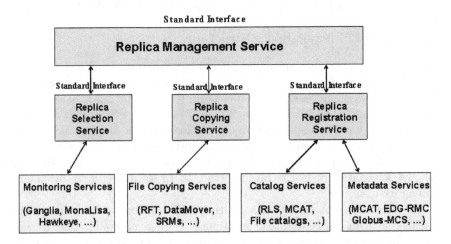

Fig. 2. Replica Management Architecture

policies, such as getting replicas only from a certain region of the world. The RMS can then invoke the RSS. The RSS's function is to order the replicas according to cost estimates of copying the physical files to the target site. In order to determine the copying costs, the RSS may consult various monitoring services. Once the physical file is selected for copying, the RMS invokes the RCS in order to copy the file to its target destination. Note that the RMS may not choose the source replica with the smallest cost. It may choose a site based on policy information about what sites to avoid (for example, to prevent bottlenecks at some sites). The RCS may use various data copying services, such as the Reliable File Transfer (RFT) service [8], Storage Resource Managers (SRMs) [9], or the DataMover [11] service that relies on SRMs. After each file is copied, the RMS can communicate with the RRS in order to register the files. Depending on the mode requested, the RRS registers the files immediately or in a delayed mode. The RRS interacts with a file catalog, a replica catalogs, and/or a meta data catalog depending on its configuration.

The orchestration between the services is mainly the coordination between copying and registration of files. As discussed above, the client should be provided with a choice of modes, such as register only if the entire multi-file copying is successful, or register only the files that were successfully copied and report failures. However, in addition to coordination between the underlying services, the RMS can be expected to provide the functionality of recovering from failures. For example, suppose that a specific physical file was selected to be copied to the target location, and that the copying failed because the file was not found (it could have been removed in the interim). The RMS can then select an alternative physical file from another site based on the information provided by the RSS. This type of functionality is expected from a well-functioning, robust, service. For this purpose one or more RRSs can be known to the RMS as part of this configuration.

5   RRS Design Considerations

In this section we outline the functionality of the Replica Registration Service. A detailed discussion of the interface can be found in [10].

The functionality of the interface specification is split into two parts, namely, the *Basic API* and *Advanced API*. The Basic API covers file registration, unregistration, and command status operations. The Advanced API introduces file attributes and name space management. A summary of the most important commands is given in Tables 1 and 2. In this paper we only discuss the design consideration of the Basic API. The Advanced API is similar to familiar file management functions and is therefore not discussed here.

5.1   Registration Functions

All the registration functions are for files only. Files can be referred to by their GUID, LFNs, or SURLs. We use the term *file references* to refer to any of these

Table 1. Basic API

Command	Explanation
Register Functions	
openCollectiveRegistration	Prepare for multiple registration calls with specific registration mode and error directive. The system returns a request token.
register	Register one or more file references using the request token.
closeCollectiveRegistration	Close a specific collective registration using the request token.
getRegistrationStatus	Retrieve information on file status (done, in progress, pending) and error codes (file not found, already exists,...).
abortRegistration	Stop registration request and unregister files.
unregister	Unregister files.
getUnregisterStatus	Retrieve status of unregister request.
Discovery Functions	
getFileReferences	Retrieve GUID, LFN and SURLs of a given file reference.
getFileReferenceStatus	Retrieve status of file reference.

Table 2. Advanced API

Command	Explanation
Attribute Functions	
getFileAttributes	Get file attributes such as *checkSum* or *fileSize*.
getFileAttributesStatus	
Name Space Management	
makeDirectory	Create a directory and register it in the catalog.
removeDirectory	Remove directory.
listDirectory	List the content of a directory.
getListDirectoryStatus	

names. All registration requests are made of pairs of file references, such as (LFN, SURL). The first item of this pair is referred to as *given* and the second item as *toBeRegistered*. For example, register (LFN, SURL) is interpreted as *for the given LFN, register the SURL*. Similarly, register (SURL, SURL) is interpreted as *for the given (first) SURL, register the (second) SURL*. In such cases, the RRS may need to get first the GUID for the existing file reference (if it is not a GUID), and then register the second file reference using the GUID. In some cases, we allow a file reference to be null, such as the first-time registration of a LFN without providing a GUID, denoted as (−, LFN). In this case, it is expected that the underlying catalog will generate the GUID. This is explained in more details in the section on first-time and subsequent registration.

Note that from the discussion above, it is obvious that all registration actions are for file references. However, in the remainder of this article we often use the term *register a file* as a short form for *register a file reference*.

Collective Registration. The RRS is designed to allow the coordination between copying and registration of files. Because copying a large number of files can be a slow process, it is necessary to allow the registration process to be a long-lasting activity. Therefore, it is necessary to have a way of specifying the beginning and the end of multiple registrations. This is achieved by starting with an openCollectiveRegistration function, followed by one or more register functions, and ending with a closeCollectiveRegistration function.

Registration Modes. As one or more files are registered, the RRS can use different modes of registration as requested by the user. A client may prefer that files be registered one-at-a-time as soon as each file is copied successfully, or may prefer to register all the files only after the entire request of copying multiple files (or entire directories) is successful. We refer to the desired behavior as the *registration mode*. Accordingly, the two registration modes supported are: *continuous* and *atEnd*. *continuous* means: register as soon as possible, and *atEnd* means: register all the files after the closeCollectiveRegistration function is called. Another advantage of this choice is that it allows the burden of accumulating the deferred registration of multiple files (until all the copying is finished) to be placed on the RRS; that is, the RRS has to accept and manage delayed registration requests. Thus, the client or the component calling the RRS does not have to save the deferred registration requests. Instead, it can pass them on to the RRS.

The implementation of the registration modes behavior depends on the target catalog. Some catalogs permit bulk registration of files, a feature that the RRS can choose to take advantage of. Some may prefer a limited number of files in the bulk registration (such as 100 at a time), and some may allow only a single file registration at-a-time. The RRS has to perform the registration as close as possible to the requested mode.

Error Directives. Registration to the underlying catalog(s) may result in unrecoverable errors. Typical errors are that a GUID, LFN or SURL is not found. For example, registering an SURL for an given LFN may result in an error that the LFN was not found, or that the SURL already exists.

Under failure conditions, clients may prefer different behaviors. We refer to this as *error directives*. These can be specified at the time the collective registration request is initiated with the openCollectiveRegistration function. Three error directives are supported:

- *stop*: register files until a non-transient error occurs and stop.
- *stopAndUndo*: register files until a non-transient error occurs, stop, and unregister all the files submitted for registration so far (undo).
- *continue*: record the error and continue registering files.

If a registration request involves thousands of files, it may be unwise to stop or undo the entire request because of a single error. It may be better to permit a few errors before the error directive gets triggered. We allow for such a parameter, called the *error directive trigger*, to be set as an integer. Regardless of whether the trigger occurs, the RRS records all such errors.

First-Time and Subsequent Registration. The registration of files into a catalog requires the distinction between a *first-time registration*, and *subsequent registrations*. During a first-time registration, a unique GUID needs to be provided by the requester, or is automatically generated by the underlying catalog GUID generation service. Some simple file catalogs use the source physical file name, that was first registered, as the GUID. In other catalogs the GUID is generated by its own *GUID generator* that guarantees a globally unique identifier. Our goal is to have a single Replica Registration Service (RRS) that can accommodate special purpose file catalogs (such as a file catalog of a scientific experiment), catalog services (such as the RLS), or other more general catalogs.

As mentioned above, all file registrations have pairs of file references, such as (LFN, SURL). For subsequent registrations the first item of this pair is referred to as *given* and the second item as *toBeRegistered*. Thus, the *given* item has to be found in the underlying catalog, while the second item should not exist. In contrast, for first-time registration, such as (GUID, LFN), both items need to be registered, and therefore both should not exist in the underlying catalog.

When a subsequent registration is requested, the RRS needs to verify that the *given* file reference is already registered. For example, a registration of a (GUID, SURL) implies that a new SURL is registered for that GUID. The RRS needs to check that the GUID already exists, and also check that the SURL does not exist. To allow full flexibility, we allow the registration of a LFN or a SURL given an existing GUID, LFN, or a SURL. This can simplify the client interaction with the RRS. For example, register (LFN, SURL) may require the client to get the GUID for the LFN first from a meta-data catalog, and then register the (GUID, SURL) to a replica catalog. The RRS is designed to save the client from having to do this extra step.

To summarize, all registration requests are made of pairs of file references. For first-time registration, the registration of (GUID, LFN) or a (GUID, SURL) implies that the first file reference, the GUID, needs to be registered as well, and therefore should not exist. In subsequent registration, the first file reference must exist and the second file reference should not exist in the underlying catalogs. The RRS relies on the underlying catalogs to verify correctness. Therefore, catalogs should provide verification of the existence of file references.

5.2   Unregister Function

The unregister function can be used to refer to a registration previously made by a collective registration request by using the request-token. The most general case is when only a request-token is provided without any specific file references. This is interpreted as *global-unregister* that means *unregister all the file reference registrations in that request*. However, since this is a global operation, and can cause serious difficulties if a mistake is made, we added a flag called *unregisterCollectiveRequest* that also has to be set. Note that we do not consider unregisterCollectiveRequest meaningful before the closeCollectiveRegistration function is called, and therefore will return an error in that case, saying *cannot unregister entire request before closeCollectiveRegistration is called.*

All the other cases to consider are requests to unregister specific file references. The specification of what to unregister can be done using pairs of file references. Similar to the subsequent *register* case, for the *unregister* function the first file reference in the pair is interpreted as *given* and the second as *toBeUnregistered*. For example, unregister (LFN, SURL) is interpreted as *for the given LFN, unregister the SURL*.

We note that a request to unregister some files can be issued while a collective registration request is in-progress (i.e. not closed yet) and therefore some of the files that need to be unregistered may still be in the RRS queue. In such a case the RRS needs to remove these requests from the queue, and unregister files that were already registered. Specifically, the RRS should suspend the collective registration process, perform the unregistration as requested, and then continue with subsequent registration requests. The same is the case after the request is closed, but the actual registration is still in-progress. The RRS needs to check the status of the request, and act accordingly.

6   Replica Registration Service in Production Use

We have implemented a Replica Registration Service (RRS) for the STAR experiment which has been used in production for over a year now. The STAR experiment [12] is a high-energy nuclear physics experiment producing real data at Brookhaven National Laboratory (BNL). The data files are replicated daily from BNL to another laboratory, Lawrence Berkeley National Laboratory (LBNL) for post-processing and analysis. The registration of the files at the LBNL site was done manually or by using scripts, a process that was prone to errors. In production, there are several thousands of files registered per month, for a total volume that averages more than 5 Terabytes.

The RRS now used in the STAR experiment automated the registration process, and practically eliminated the error rates (from about 1% to 0.02%), according to the person in charge of the replication operation [5]. The RRS was implemented as a daemon module that listens for information provided by the component responsible to replicate the files, called a DataMover [11]. The DataMover interacts with two Storage Resource Managers (SRMs), one at the source site (BNL) and one at the target site (LBNL). When the target SRM receives a file and archives it, it notifies the RRS. It is the responsibility of the RRS to register the files. The registration is made to a STAR file catalog (which uses a relational database, MySQL), by invoking a script. The production setup is shown in Figure 3.

The RRS was implemented having three modes: *continuous*, *every-n-files*, and *at-end*. In the *continuous mode*, the RRS tries to register each file immediately. In the *every-n-files mode*, the RRS queues the registration requests until it has n files, and then registers then n files in a single *bulk* registration. In the *at-end mode*, the RRS waits till the replication of the *entire set* of files is successful, and only then registers them. Another function of the RRS is to make sure that successful registration occurs when the File Catalog is temporarily unavailable. If the File Catalog is busy or down, the RRS keeps trying periodically until the registration is successful. This alleviates the burden from the client of having to keep track of successful registrations. Initially we experimented with the *every-n-files mode* of registration. However, we found that in this application of large-scale continuous replication, the *continuous mode* was effective as the *every-n-files mode*.

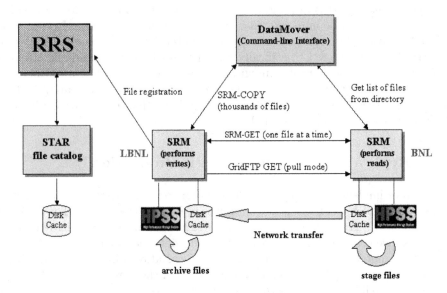

Fig. 3. Replica Registration Service used in production for a physics experiment

It is worth mentioning that we considered the option of having the RRS being a client that *pulls* the information from the SRM, but this design would require the RRS to poll the SRM continuously. We chose, instead, to implement the RRS as a daemon, so that the SRM can *push* the information to the RRS. This reduced the communication overhead significantly. However, a more general replication service may choose to *poll* the SRM or the target storage system, and then notify the RRS of files that were already transferred.

The RRS was designed to interact with various catalogs, where most of the code is reusable and only the request to register files changes depending on the target catalog. By having a uniform interface it should be possible to replace one catalog by another if necessary without effecting the client programs.

In general, a Virtual Organization (VO) can use multiple RRS services. The coordination between these RRS services must be done by the RMS layer according to their configuration for keeping track of file assignments to storage systems. However, this is a VO issue that is beyond the scope of this paper.

7   Conclusions

In this paper we introduced the Replica Registration Service (RRS) that provides a uniform interface to various file catalogs, replica catalogs, and meta data catalogs. The RRS supports collective file registration requests and keeps persistent registration queues for large-scale usage where thousands of files are registered. The RRS also supports a set of error directives that are triggered in case of registration failures. This work is a first step toward standardizing the access of file and replica catalogs to allow interchangeability of such systems.

Acknowledgment

We want to thank Jean-Philippe Baud, James Casey, Ann Chervenak, Peter Kunszt, Reagan Moore, and Robert Schuler for their comments on the specification and possible extensions of the RRS interface. We also thank Viji Natarajan for providing the current implementation. This work was supported by the Director, Office of Science, Office of Advanced Scientific Computing, of the U.S. Department of Energy under Contract No. DE-AC03-76SF00098.

References

1. C. Baru, R. Moore, A. Rajasekar, and M. Wan. The SDSC Storage Research Broker. In *CASCON'98*, Toronto, Canada, 30 November - 3 December 1998.
2. J.-P. Baud and J. Casey. Evolution of LCG-2 Data Management. In *Computing in High Energy Physics*, Interlaken, Switzerland, September 2004.
3. A. Chervenak, E. Deelman, I. Foster, L. Guy, A. Iamnitchi, C. Kesselman, W. Hoschek, M. Ripeanu, B. Schwartzkopf, H. Stockinger, K. Stockinger, and B. Tierney. Giggle: A Framework for Constructing Scalable Replica Location Services. In *Super Computing 2002*, Baltimore, USA, November 2002.
4. A. Chervenak, I. Foster, C. Kesselman, and C. Salisburyand S. Tuecke. The Data Grid: Towards an Architecture for the Distributed Management and Analysis of Large Scientific Datasets. *Journal of Network and Computer Applications*, 23, 2001.
5. PPDG Collaboration. Physics results from the STAR experiment at RHIC benefit from production Grid data services. http://www.ppdg.net/docs/oct04/ppdg-star-oct04.pdf.
6. P. Kunszt et al. EGEE gLite User's Guide - Overview of gLite Data Management. Technical Report EGEE-TECH-570643-v1.0, CERN, Geneva, Switzerland, March 2005.
7. P. Kunszt, E. Laure, H. Stockinger, and K. Stockinger. File-based Replica Management . *Future Generation Computer Systems*, 22(1), 2005.
8. R. Madduri, C. Hood, and W. Allcock. Reliable File Transfers in Grid Environments. In *27th IEEE Conference on Local Computer Networks*, Tampa, Florida, November 6 - 8 2002.
9. A. Shoshani, A. Sim, and J. Gu. Storage Resource Managers: Essential Components for the Grid. In *Grid Resource Management: State of the Art and Future Trends*, 2003. Edited by J. Nabrzyski, J. M. Schopf, J. Weglarz, Kluwer Academic Publishers.

10. A. Shoshani, A. Sim, and K. Stockinger. Replica Registration Service - Functional Interface Specification 1.0. Berkeley Lab, Berkeley, California, April 2005.
11. A. Sim, J. Gu, A. Shoshani, and V. Natarajan. DataMover: Robust Terabyte-Scale Multi-file Replication over Wide-Area Networks. In *Scientific and Statistical Database Management*, Santorini Island, Greece, June 2004.
12. The STAR Experiment. http://www.star.bnl.gov/.
13. H. Stockinger, A. Samar, B. Allcock, I. Foster, K. Holtman, and B. Tierney. File and Object Replication in Data Grids. *Journal of Cluster Computing*, 5(3), 2002.

Datagridflows: Managing Long-Run Processes on Datagrids

Arun Jagatheesan[1,2], Jonathan Weinberg[1], Reena Mathew[1], Allen Ding[1],
Erik Vandekieft[1], Daniel Moore[1,3], Reagan Moore[1], Lucas Gilbert[1],
Mark Tran[1], and Jeffrey Kuramoto[1]

[1] San Diego Supercomputer Center,
University of California, San Diego,
9500 Gilman Drive, MC0505, La Jolla, CA 92093
{arun, jonw, alding, moore, iktome, kuramoto}@sdsc.edu
{rmathew, evandeki}@cs.ucsd.edu
mixx@umail.ucsb.edu
mdtran@ucsd.edu
[2] Institute of High Energy Physics and Astrophysics,
University of Florida,
Gainesville, FL 32611
[3] Department of Computer Science,
University of California, Santa Barbara, CA93106

Abstract. This paper is an introduction to *Datagridflows*. Until recently, datagrids were generally considered over-hyped and the associated technologies not widely embraced in the academic community. Today, datagrids have become a reality and an important technology for managing large, unstructured data and storage resources distributed over autonomous administrative domains. The datagrids that are operating in production provide us an idea of new requirements and challenges that will be faced in future datagrid environments. One such requirement is the coordinated execution of long-run data management processes in datagrids. We term these processes as "datagridflows". This new area provides exciting opportunities and challenges to researchers in distributed computing and distributed databases. This paper is intended to introduce these challenges to other researchers, including those new to grid computing. We provide motivation through discussion of datagridflow requirements and real production scenarios. We introduce current work on datagridflow technologies including the *Datagrid Language (DGL)* for describing datagridflows in datagrids.

1 Introduction

Datagrid technology is currently used for managing very large, unstructured data storage resources [1, 2, 3]. The need for long-run data management processes on top of datagrid environments is seen as a common emerging requirement in most datagrid deployments. Examples of these long-run processes include datagrid information lifecycle management, datagrid triggers, and data-intensive computational workflows. These long-run processes could be considered "datagrid workflows" and are discussed later in this paper. We refer to these long-run datagrid processes as datagridflows.

J.-M. Pierson (Ed.): VLDB DMG 2005, LNCS 3836, pp. 113–128, 2005.

In the following section, we introduce some fundamental concepts in datagrids for the benefit of those new to grid computing. In section 2, we describe three motivating scenarios for datagridflows and our work on the Data Grid Language. We discuss the requirements and components of a system to manage datagridflows in section 3. In section 4, we provide some overview of our work on the Data Grid Language as part of the SRB Matrix Project. Related and future works to this paper are presented in section 5.

1.1 Data Grid Landscape

In this section, we introduce datagrids, associated concepts and relevant terminology to prepare the reader for the problem statement discussed in the following sections.

Grid Computing. We describe a "grid" as a coordinated distributed computing infrastructure, formed by combining heterogeneous resources from autonomous administrative domains. Grids provide the infrastructure that is used for large-scale, resource-intensive, and distributed applications. The definition of a Grid is continually evolving as different people have different perspectives of the same technology. The commonality that is observed in the different perspectives of the "Grid" is the formation of a logical infrastructure as a single ensemble, by dynamically combining independently managed resources.

Datagrid. A datagrid is a logical unified view of a grid's data storage infrastructure. Data storage middleware create a federated, location independent, logical infrastructure namespace that dynamically spreads across the grid's administrative domains. Datagrids support sharing data collections and storage resources between autonomous administrative domains. A shared collection is a logical aggregation of digital entities, (e.g.) files, which are physically distributed in multiple physical storage resources that are owned by multiple administrative domains. A shared resource allows users from multiple administrative domains to share data storage space. The core concept behind the success for datagrid software is the concept of "data virtualization".

Data Virtualization. Data Virtualization is the concept of bringing together different heterogeneous data and storage resources into one or more *logical views* so that the distributed and replicated data appear as a single logical data source managed by a single data management system. This logical view is simple for users and applications as it hides the complexity of working with distributed and heterogeneous systems. The logical view is provided on top of a logical resource namespace, allowing high levels of flexibility for distributed computing and migration of data storage resources. Data and resource names are logical and can be physically changed or migrated without affecting the applications. The underlying concept behind the datagrids and data virtualization is the same as the concept behind relational databases: *to isolate physical organization of the data from logical schema.* In data virtualization, we go one step further. Instead of completely hiding the physical organization of the storage resources where the data resides, another logical namespace of storage resources is provided to the applications. Applications now have the added capability to perform distributed data management operations on the combined logical data namespace along with logical resource namespace without having to directly interact with the physical storage resources or the physical organization of data.

There has been a significant increase in use of datagrid technology over the past few years. Data storage infrastructures using datagrid technologies are deployed in many countries. Much of the data managed by these technologies is in the form of files. One of the popular datagrid management systems (DGMS) [1], the SDSC Storage Resource Broker (SRB) [2], is believed to broker around a Petabyte of data worldwide at the time of this writing.

Multiple independent organizations deploy the SRB middleware on top of their existing physical storage resources without any changes to the existing system. The existing physical storage resources are represented in the SRB datagrid namespace as logical storage resources. Each SRB storage server that runs on top of a physical storage system maps that particular physical storage system into the data grid logical resource namespace. Many organizations participate in a data grid. Users can view and use the resources of users from other organizations given appropriate access permissions and authentication mechanisms. Users use any logical resource from the data grid logical resource namespace using the SRB protocol without even knowing where the resource is physically located or what type of physical storage resource is actually used. In addition, users can create an aggregated logical view of distributed data in the form of shared collections, enabling them to have the same logical namespace or data organization even if when the data is moved. Thus, the data namespace or the logical view of the data in the grid is independent of infrastructure and location information for the end users.

2   Long-Run Processes in Datagrids

The widespread use of datagrids has helped us observe several common usage patterns in datagrid environments that require long-run datagrid processes. In this section, we present the three prominent patterns that we have observed. These motivate our work on datagridflows.

2.1   Data Grid ILM

Information Lifecycle Management (ILM), as described in the data storage industry, refers to the dynamic re-orientation of data placement and data retention strategies based on storage cost and the "business value" of the data to be managed. The term "business value of data" refers to the value certain data or information provides to the business requirements. Unlike traditional Hierarchical Storage Management (HSM) solutions, which normally use "data freshness" as the most important attribute in determining data placement, ILM solutions use data value and business policies to determine data placement and retention. It must be mentioned that in most business cases a high value of data freshness will automatically yield a high business value for the data. Hence, ILM could be considered an extension of HSM.

In a datagrid, information in the form of several related data collections would have a lifecycle that spans multiple organizations. Information in the datagrid could be created by one organization, accessed or replicated by other organizations, and archived at yet another organization before finally being deleted from the datagrid.

During its lifecycle, information in the grid would have different business values for different domains participating in the datagrid. This value is based on the needs of a particular domain's users and the role played by that domain in the data grid. For example, data being created might be of interest to the domain that is creating it. Later, some other domain in the data grid might have more value for the same information. We refer this as domain-specific value as "domain value". Organizations could create replicas of the same data in their own domains as the domain value of certain data grows. Once a domain's users are not interested in some information, its domain value decreases and data can either be deleted or migrated to less expensive storage systems. A change to data storage organization with respect to domain value of some information is called a "datagrid ILM processes". These changes usually do not involve any transformation of data. They could involve replication, migration or removal of existing data, changing access permissions on some data before they are migrated or archived, etc.,

In addition to changes in the domain users' interest in information that could initiate the ILM processes, the role played by a domain in the datagrid could also initiate ILM processes. In some cases, one of the domain's roles in the data grid could be just to archive all or some selected information in the datagrid. This could be a third-party service provider or an IT department for the enterprise responsible for archiving data. The archiver domain might not have any real users who are interested in the information – but its business processes are interested in archiving the information. The archiver domain could store the information for years, before finally moving it the lowest cost data storage system from a long-term storage management perspective. The archiver domain could be an example for what we refer to as an "imploding star". Information from all the domains in the datagrid is finally pulled towards this domain. This certainly involves a very well planned archival schedule. An example for this type of imploding star is the BBSRC-CCLRC data grid [3]. In the BBSRC project, information from multiple hospitals in United Kingdom are finally archived into an archiver site.

The complement of the imploding star based datagrid ILM is the "exploding star". In this case, information is pushed or replicated outside the domain of its creation. For example, the datagrid created for the CMS High Energy Physics experiment at CERN has many domains that require the data generated by the CMS experiment to be replicated in stages at different tiers across the globe. The CERN domain thus acts as the exploding star. Domains can play other roles such as a "data curator" role in a digital library that is powered using the data grid technology.

We can observe some commonalities and generic requirements in these datagrid ILMs. All of them require long-run processes on top of the datagrid namespaces. These long-run processes could be started, stopped and restarted at any time. For example, an ILM process could only be run at some domains during non-working hours or on weekends. This would require powerful and highly flexible systems to manage these datagrid ILM processes. A requirement from digital libraries and persistent archives, like the National Archives Persistent Archives Test bed (NARA PAT) [4] is to preserve the provenance information associated with these ILM processes. The requirement is to enable the storing of provenance information for not only the

DGMS operations performed by the system, but also the operations that are performed as part of the archival pipeline.

Currently, some simple datagrid ILM processes can be implemented using simple scripts and cron jobs on some operating systems. System administrators are familiar with these scripts. However, once the requirements include multiple domains, multiple system administrators and multiple ILM processes, more sophisticated systems are required to handle problem. The proposed new systems for datagrid ILM must support:

- Start, stop, pause and restart of datagrid ILM Processes
- Query the status of the any datagrid ILM any time
- Provenance information of all the processes managed at any time even (years) after the execution
- Programmatic API to define these datagrid ILM and programmatic interface for interaction by other systems
- Programmatic API to query and monitor any step in the datagrid ILM process

One major requirement is to provide an interoperable description of the datagrid ILM processes. A standard format could be used across all the related systems like datagrids, grid file systems, digital libraries, persistent archives and dataflow systems. Such a standard based on an XML Schema would allow programmatic interaction of all the systems. The proposed XML schema must support the definition of ILM processes of various complexities. The schema must describe all relevant entities, including data, resources, and users. The schema would have to be programmatically described and executed dynamically as the constraints associated with these processes are dynamically modified.

2.2 Datagrid Triggers

The datagrid namespace is a logical view of data and storage resources. A datagrid trigger is a mapping from any event in the logical data storage namespace to a process initiated in the datagrid in response to such an event. Datagrid triggers are defined on top of the datagrid namespace and could have the following components.

Event. An event could be any change in the datagrid namespace including updates, inserts, and deletes. Datagrid triggers could be triggered before or after events complete. Unlike database transactions datagrid processes or not transactional. The results of applying the trigger-based mechanisms on this non-transactional, large-scale, distributed data management system have not yet been studied.

Condition. Trigger execution is determined by the evaluation of some state information in the datagrid. This is very similar to the database Event-Condition-Action (ECA rules) based processing used in database rules.

Actions. An Action is the execution any data management process on the datagrid namespace. Multiple actions could be performed based on the evaluation of the condition associated with the trigger.

Datagrid triggers will play an important role for managing unstructured data in datagrids. Simple use-cases include: creating metadata when a file is created, sending notifications when specific types of files are ingested, and automating replication of certain data based on their meta-data.

Datagrids allow user-defined metadata to be associated with data. Triggers could make use of these parameters. There are many open research issues here. Datagrid management systems (DGMS's) [1] will allow multiple users to define triggers. Different results might be produced based on the order in which triggers defined by multiple users are processed for the same event. Further complicating the situation is the non-transactional nature of datagrid processes.

In databases, the Structured Query Language (SQL or PL/SQL) can describe the triggers and the DBMS executes associated actions. A similar language is required for DGMS's to describe triggers with respect to files, the metadata that are associated with those files, data collections, data storage resources, etc. Such a language should support data types such as collections and datasets. The proposed language could also be used to describe constructs in datagrids similar to "stored procedures" in databases. This will allow the datagrid stored procedures to be run from the DGMS itself rather than executing the procedure outside the DGMS using client side components. We introduce "Data Grid Language" (DGL) as a possible solution for this later in this paper.

2.3 Data-Intensive Workflows

The last motivation that we want to mention regarding long-run processes in datagrids is the use of the datagrid infrastructure to perform scientific or computational workflows on unstructured data. Such workflows are sometimes referred to as "scientific workflows" because they are often used in certain scientific applications, but the associated concepts apply equally for non-scientific workflows that require intensive processing.

Grid-workflow is the automation of a business process whereby data and tasks are passed from one grid-participant to another according to some set of procedural rules. A single grid workflow process could have multiple tasks that might have to be executed at different domains participating in the grid. The dynamic scheduling of these tasks to the different participating domains could be based on the combined cost all the tasks together at different domains. The cost of executing each task at a domain could be based on multiple parameters including the amount of data moved, the number of CPU cycles that would be left idle in the grid, the clock time taken to execute all the tasks, the bandwidth utilized, etc. The cost is just an approximate value based on certain heuristics used by the scheduler.

During their execution, Grid-workflows must consider different logics: the business process logic, the execution logic and the infrastructure logic as explained below.

Business Logic. Business logic is a representation of the specific business task that takes part in the workflow. Some examples of business logic are: processing an order-entry form (e-business), determining a document type while archiving it in the prototype for National Archives Workflow (document management), or any transformation used in scientific pipelines (scientific workflow). The isolation of the business logic from the complexities involved in datagrid computing provides ease of development of the business logic. The business logic development team need not be concerned with scaling up its solution or taking advantage of the distributed nature of the datagrid. They should only be required to describe the requirements in terms of resource types and the service levels required to execute the business logic. Business logic is usually in the form of binary executables that could be run on appropriate platforms in the datagrid.

Infrastructure Logic. Infrastructure Logic refers to the logic that has to be used while matching the tasks in the workflow with the appropriate resources and domains within the grid infrastructure. Infrastructure logic would involve the description of available resources in the infrastructure, the service level agreements (SLAs) the resources can support, the preferred type of users or tasks that could be executed on each resources, etc. Infrastructure logic could also involve heuristics that are supposed to be used by a Datagridflow Management System (DfMS) while scheduling the tasks to the different resources in different domains.

The DfMS would have to map the requirement of each business logic task to the appropriate resources required. The workflow description would dictate what types of resource are required at what SLAs. The description might be just a logical or abstract specification of the type of resource required rather than a specific physical system. This allows dynamic binding to a particular resource at runtime. The workflow description is used by DfMS along with Grid Resource Brokers to bind the task with appropriate resources. For example, the workflow description might logically specify that a particular task would require an archival system, a high-performance file system, or a certain number of compute nodes. Infrastructure logic on the other hand, would specify the mapping from these logical resource types with the physical endpoints and the SLAs that can be supported. The system administrators could change the infrastructure logic based on their own domain requirements, assuring them full autonomous control over what resources are shared with other grid users and at what SLAs.

Execution Logic. Execution logic provides the control-flow and ordering of tasks that take part in the workflow. Execution Logic is provided by the end-user or the workflow designer. It provides a description of the workflow execution, identifying the tasks that take part in the workflow, the order in which they should be executed, the relationship among them, their input and output data sets, etc.

Execution logic also has information on the state of execution. This information can be checked before execution of any process. Fault handling information for the processes could also be provided in the execution logic. Execution logic could remain independent of the infrastructure dependencies allowing late binding of resources. However, a workflow designer could still choose to specify a particular resource instead of leaving it abstract to be bound later.

Execution logic also captures the requirement to run tasks for a specified number of times or until some milestone is reached. This is very useful in datagrids where the workflow involves iterating some set of tasks over collections of files. The files are used as input data and processed according to a datagrid query, which could be part of the execution logic itself. This allows configuration of runtime parameters by changing the execution logic rather than configuring the business logic and recompiling the associated code. The execution logic could be viewed as the abstract definition of a workflow without concrete descriptions of the underlying physical infrastructure.

Infrastructure-based Execution Logic. The Execution Logic is converted dynamically into Infrastructure-based Execution Logic just before the execution of the tasks that are described in the workflow. This is a multi-stage hierarchical process. An analogy for this process could be the query re-writing or optimization of SQL before a final query plan is generated and executed by the databases. The description of the execution logic is rewritten into infrastructure-specific execution logic based on multiple factors including: the requirements of the task, availability of resources, the physical locations of the input or output data, the presence of "virtual data" [5] or "virtual services" [6] and other infrastructure heuristics.

Iterations or milestones present in the execution logic would require a small section in the description of the execution logic, a group of tasks, to be dynamically converted into infrastructure-based execution logic multiple times. The group of tasks, a small section of the execution logic for a single iteration, would have to be dynamically converted into infrastructure-based execution logic very late in the processes just before execution. This late binding allows execution of the each iteration at a different location based on the infrastructure availability just before the tasks are executed.

The scheduling or selection of the appropriate resources for each task has to choose the location for execution of a task based on: the available physical locations of input data (replicas), desired physical location of the output data, location of the business logic (code) and the available resources where the task can be executed. If the required output data is already available (virtual data), it need not be derived again. The final infrastructure-based execution logic for each task would have the chosen replica to use as input, the location of the output data and the grid resource to use. In a datagrid, the replica selection could be handled by the DGMS itself based on location of execution of the process.

All the execution logic associated with the Grid-workflow must be generated programmatically and exchanged among the participating resources. This includes the datagrid execution logic and infrastructure-based execution logic. The Data Grid Language described in the following sections could be used for to describe these sets of logic. Even though multiple workflow languages are already available, the existence of datagrid-related data types and operations as part of the language itself makes it the suitable language to describe these grid-based data-intensive processes that take part in scientific workflows.

In this section, we have surveyed three of our major motivating scenarios in detail and their requirements with respect to datagrid technology. One common observation from all these scenarios is the need for datagridflows on top of datagrid systems. Another requirement that has been mentioned in all the scenarios is the need for a language to describe the long-run processes in the datagrid. In the next section, we introduce Datagridflows and their requirements.

3 Datagridflows

Datagridflow is the automation of a long run process whereby data and/or tasks are passed from one datagrid participant to another according to a set of procedural rules. Datagridflows are data-intensive long run processes like datagrid ILM, datagrid triggers, or computational workflows in a datagrid environment. Datagridflows could be viewed as a subset of regular workflows that involve long-run processes on datagrids. Most of the data processed is unstructured, file-like data.

Workflow systems have been around for many years. There are many ways to hard-wire workflows and develop a system that uniquely satisfies a single user's requirement. This approach is easy for the developers to begin with as they can use any of their favorite programming languages to hard-wire the tasks involved in the workflow. However, from a long-term perspective, this approach is not optimal and it becomes extremely expensive to maintain the code that supports the whole system. Any change in the execution logic or the infrastructure logic would require modification of the whole system. A generic system would be useful for the datagrid community, which has clear needs to manage datagridflows, as can be seen in multiple projects including National Archives Persistent Archive Test bed Project [4], Southern California Earthquake Center [7], CCLRC-BBSRC project [3] and LLNL UCSD SciData Management Pipeline.

3.1 Generic Requirements for a Datagridflow Management System (DfMS)

The challenge is to provide a generic system that can manage most of the datagridflow requirements faced by these data-intensive projects. The common patterns that we observe from our users' requirements when they want to manage their datagridflows:

- *Data-intensive flows:* Most of the projects that use datagrid technology usually have large data collections. DfMS must take full advantage of the underlying DGMS software that provides all the functions required to manage the very large unstructured data.
- *Scalability:* DfMS must be scalable in terms of the number of tasks within a single workflow; number of workflows that can be processed, and the number of resources the workflows can physically take advantage of to complete a workflow.
- *Collections and Files:* Most of the data that is processed in a DfMS is in the form of collections and files. DfMS's must support these data types and the operations that can be supported on collections and files in a datagrid.
- *Highly Flexible:* Most of these projects will deploy the DfMS in production for at least five years. Over this time, many requirements, probably unknown during requirements analysis, will emerge. The system should therefore be flexible to handle new requirements.
- *Cost of Operation:* Having one more software system to manage increases the Total Cost of Operation (TCO) of the project. DfMS must minimize the maintenance requirements and the system administrator should not have a need to learn another system.

- *Provenance:* DfMS must have manage information about all workflows and their tasks. This information would be queried and audited later.
- *Novice and Expert Users:* DfMS must have a GUI-based system to interact with novice users and an API based interface for developers and expert users to programmatically interact with the DfMS
- *Distributed Grid Infrastructure:* DfMS must take advantage of the distributed grid infrastructure while executing its operations
- *Task Granularity:* Workflow designers should have the flexibility to design datagridflows with each task that is not too small and not too large to be called a task.

The above requirements are generic for both business and academic/scientific workflows. Similar business use cases would be observed once business users start using datagrids and the Grid File System (GFS) [9].

3.2 Components of a Datagridflow System

The following are the components of a hypothetical Datagridflow System from a high-level perspective.

Datagridflow IDE (GUI). A Datagridflow modeling interface would serve as an Integrated Development Environment (IDE) for end-users to interact with the DfMS. A modeling markup language describes datagridflows and stores it locally for the users to use again or view the datagridflow rendered on the IDE. MoML [8], used in Ptolemy II/Kepler uses, this approach to serve as a datagridflow IDE.

Datagrid Language (DGL). A language to describe, query, and manage execution logic and infrastructure-based execution logic. The SRB Matrix uses this approach. A DGL document could be created by the IDE and sent to the DfMS server for processing. More on DGL is provided in the next section.

DfMS Server. The DfMS server can service DGL requests both synchronously and asynchronously. DfMS server manages state information about all the tasks, which can be queried at any time. The DfMS server works on top of the datagrid server (DGMS) and can support the datagrid operations provided by DGMS. In the SRB Matrix project [10], the *Matrix* Server uses SRB as its DGMS. Multiple DfMS servers can form a peer-to-peer datagridflow network with one or more lookup servers. DfMS servers could have additional capabilities to directly interact with the DGMS server, allowing the users to create Datagrid Triggers and Datagrid ILM jobs at the DGMS it self. The DfMS server can provide the concepts of virtual data by incorporating a virtual data system as a component. The GriPhyN Chimera System is an example of such a component that could be present in the DfMS server.

Infrastructure Description Language. The Infrastructure Description Language describes the infrastructure at each domain and the different SLAs they can support. Infrastructure includes data storage resources, compute resources, DGMS server location etc.

Grid Schedulers and Brokers. Grid schedulers and brokers act as intermediaries, that do the planning and matchmaking between the appropriate tasks in a workflow with the resources that are available. They are used to convert the abstract execution logic into concrete infrastructure-based execution logic. Tools are available for planning and scheduling on the grid. One such tool is the GriPhyN Pegasus planner [11].

4   The Data Grid Language

We have discussed the need for a datagrid language as part of our motivating scenarios. Just as SQL is used for databases, an analog is needed for datagrids. Our contribution to the datagridflows and the datagrid community is the *Datagrid Language* (DGL), which is useful for all of our motivating scenarios. DGL is an XML-Schema specification that can be extended for domain-specific operations and used by any community.

DGL explicitly supports data types such as datagrid collections, files and datagrid operations as part of the language it self. This enables the description of file-based flows and datagrid collection processing. DGL can be used to describe datagridflow processes, queries, and status. The language is designed to work with a protocol based on a request-response model. In addition to request-response, DGL can also be used with one-way messages also. The requests can be synchronous or asynchronous.

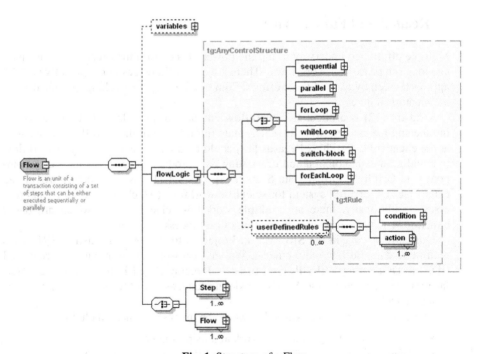

Fig. 1. Structure of a Flow

DGL describes each task of a datagridflow as a "Step" with associated input and output parameters. One or more steps are aggregated into "Flows", which are recursive control structures that describe how to execute steps. Each flow is like a block of code in modern programming languages with its own variable scope, commands, and steps. Each flow defines a unique control pattern that dictates how its contents should be executed, e.g. sequentially, in parallel, while loop, for-each loop, switch-case, etc. These patterns are very similar to any modern programming language. Using these control structures recursively, users can create arbitrarily complicated gridflow descriptions. Figure 1 shows the schema definition for a flow in DGL.

Each DGL transaction generates a unique identifier that can be used to query the status of the any task in the workflow at any level of granularity. The identifier for any particular task or flow can be shared with all other processes that require access to the status of the particular task or flow.

DGL also supports user-defined, Event-Condition-Action rules. This enables an event-based model for datagridflow programming. More information about DGL can be found in Appendix A of this document.

DGL has been used in prototype runs for managing datagridflows at the UCSD Libraries and SCEC Project. Datagridflow for data-integrity and MD5 calculation was described in DGL and executed by SRB Matrix servers for the UCSD Library data. SCEC workflow for ingesting files into the SRB datagrid was also performed using DGL [14].

5   Related and Future Work

Multiple efforts are underway to tap the power of the grid infrastructure and to manage long run process or workflows. There are clear differences in the objective and/or approach taken by each of these efforts. Some of the projects working in related areas are mentioned here.

GridAnt [12] is a client-side workflow engine that provides scripting support to initiate and manage the workflow. The state information of the workflow is managed at the client side. GriPhyN Pegasus [11] could be used as planner in a grid workflow to avoid redundant computation of existing data products. Pegasus is used as a component in GriPhyN Virtual Data System [5]. Kepler [13] is an effort to provide an extensible IDE and full system for scientific workflow (which are also long run processes). Additionally, there are multiple workflow related efforts, which are based either on Web/Grid Service Composition or on Process Ordering.

Our current work in the SRB Matrix Project is to support our existing SRB users with these datagridflow requirements. We are also working on providing a rich GUI (IDE) to DGL using VERGIL GUI (used in Ptolemy II and Kepler). The user interface will be defined by the MoML modeling language, with execution taking place using the DGL.

There are many research issues that would be interest to others, including:

- Peer-to-peer datagridflow network and its protocols
- Distributed data scheduling for datagrid ILM policy strategies for enterprises
- Dynamic datagrid scheduling based on heuristics at different domains

Datagridflows is an emerging field that presents some exciting challenges. Datagrid users already require powerful peer-to-peer datagridflow networks. More work would help the community understand more about the requirement and the usefulness of different approaches taken.

6 Conclusions

Datagridflow is an emerging field that supports the proliferation of datagrid technology by addressing the new requirements of datagrid users. Datagridflows enable users to automate or semi-automate tasks in the datagrid. Many more challenges and opportunities are present for researchers from distributed computing and distributed databases.

Acknowledgement

This work was supported by NSF GriPhyN, NPACI REU and SDSC REU. We would like to acknowledge Peter Berrisford of CCLRC, UK; David Little, UCSD Libraries; and Marcio Faerman and Phil Macheling of the SCEC project for providing us descriptions of their datagridflows requirements in their projects.

References

1. Moore, R.W., Jagatheesan, A., Rajasekar, A., Wan, M. and Schroeder, W., "Data Grid Management Systems," *Proceedings of the 21st IEEE/NASA Conference on Mass Storage Systems and Technologies*, 2004, Maryland.
2. Rajasekar, A., Wan, M., Moore, R.W., Jagatheesan, A. and Kremenek, G., "Real Experiences with Data Grids – Case-studies in using the SRB," Proceedings of 6th International Conference/Exhibition on High Performance Computing Conference in Asia Pacific Region (HPC-Asia), December 2002, Bangalore, India
3. BBSRC-CCLRC Data Grid. Web site: (http://www.e-science.clrc.ac.uk/web/projects/bbsrc_grid_support)
4. Archivist Grid Website: http://www.sdsc.edu/Press/2004/04/040904_PersistenArchives.html
5. Foster, I., Voeckler, J., Wilde, M. and Zhao, Y., "Chimera: A Virtual Data System for Representing, Querying, and Automating Data Derivation". In Scientific and Statistical Database Management, (2002).
6. Jagatheesan, A., Moore, R., Rajasekar, A. and Zhu, B., "Virtual Services in Data Grids", In the 11th IEEE International Symposium on High Performance Distributed Computing (HPDC), July 2002, Scotland.
7. Southern California Earthquake Center, SCEC: http://www.scec.org/cme
8. Edward A. Lee and Steve Neuendorffer. *MoML — A Modeling Markup Language in XML — Version 0.4*. Technical report, University of California at Berkeley, March, 2000
9. Arun Jagatheesan, "Architecture of Grid File System", Gridforge. https://forge.gridforum.org/projects/gfs-wg
10. SRB Matrix Website: http://www.sdsc.edu/srb/matrix

11. E. Deelman, J. Blythe, Y. Gil, C. Kesselman, G. Mehta, S. Patil, M. Su, K. Vahi and M. Livny , "Pegasus: Mapping scientific workflows onto the grid," Across Grids Conference 2004, Nicosia, Cyprus.

12. Kaizar Amin and Gregor von Laszewski, GridAnt: A Grid Workflow System. Manual, February 2003 http://www-unix.globus.org/cog/projects/gridant/

13. B. Ludäscher, I. Altintas, C. Berkley, D. Higgins, E. Jaeger-Frank, M. Jones, E. Lee, J. Tao, Y. Zhao, "Scientific Workflow Management and the Kepler System", Concurrency and Computation: Practice & Experience, Special Issue on Scientific Workflows.

14. Weinberg, J., Jagatheesan, A., Ding, A., Fareman, M. and Hu, Y., "Gridflow Description, Query, and Execution at SCEC using the SDSC Matrix, " Proceedings of the 13th IEEE International Symposium on High-Performance Distributed Computing (HPDC), June 4-6, 2004, Honolulu, Hawaii, USA.

Appendix

A Structure of DGL

A DGL document is a XML based description that could be either a *Data Grid Request* or *Data Grid Response*. A Data Grid Request is sent from a client to the DfMS server. Currently, the DfMS server uses a request-response paradigm and replies with a Data Grid Response for each request.

Figure 2 shows the structure of a Data Grid Request. It contains general information including: Document metadata, Grid user information and the Virtual Organization to which the user belongs. The Data Grid Request's core component is either a *Flow* or a *FlowStatusQuery*. A *Flow* describes a workflow to be executed and a *FlowStatusQuery* is a query on the status of execution of a *Flow* at any granular level.

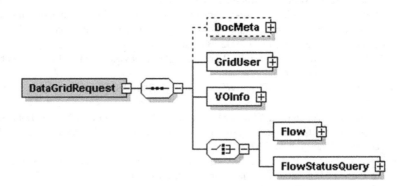

Fig. 2. Structure of a DataGridRequest

The *Flow* is a recursive data structure that represents the gridflow execution. It contains more recursive *Flow*s or *Step*s (called its "children"). Abstractly, we can think of a *Flow* as an execution environment or a block of code that sets up a scope and behavior for its children execute (e.g. sequentially, in parallel, for-loop, etc).

As shown in Figure 1, each *Flow* contains three sections:

- *Variables* – A *Flow* can declare any number of variables for use in its scope
- *FlowLogic* – This component dictates the logic by which the contents should be executed (e.g. sequentially, in parallel, etc)
- *Children* – Sub-flows or steps (but not both), which will be executed within this *Flow*'s scope according to its *FlowLogic*.

FlowLogic

The *FlowLogic* element contains two sections: the first is a choice of control structure (e.g. sequential, parallel, etc) that dictates how the children of this *Flow* will be executed. The second is a set of *UserDefined Rules* that encapsulate the actions that the *Flow* should take upon starting up and before exiting. Figure 3 shows the *Flow-Logic* schema.

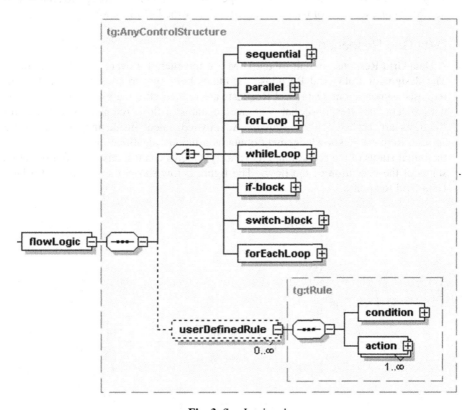

Fig. 3. flowLogic schema

Before it starts execution, a *Flow* will execute the user-defined rule named "beforeEntry" if one is defined in its *FlowLogic*. After finishing execution, it will execute the rule "afterExit" if one is defined.

User Defined Rule

A *UserDefinedRule* is similar to a switch statement in programming languages. A *UserDefinedRule* consists of a condition and one or more action statements. The condition is represented using *tCondition*. *Tcondition* is a usually simple string that is evaluated. It is possible to use DGL variables in the Tcondition. Each *UserDefinedRule* has one condition and can have one ore more Actions. Each action has a (string) name associated with it. The Actions are executed if the condition statement evaluates to the name of the action.

Step

A *Step* is a concrete action that a gridflow performs. A *Step* can declare variables and *userDefinedRules* just like a *Flow*, but contains a single element called an *Operation*. The operation describes some atomic operation that the gridflow is to execute. DGL supports a number of DataGrid related operations for SDSC's Storage Resource Broker (SRB) or execution of business logic (code) by the DfMS server.

Data Grid Response

A Data Grid Response is sent by the DfMS to the client for every Data Grid Request. The design for Data Grid Response facilitates both synchronous and asynchronous requests. Synchronous Data Grid Requests are replied after the execution of the flow with a Data Grid Response that contains the status of flow. Asynchronous Data Grid Requests are replied with a Request Acknowledgement inside the Data Grid Response. Request Acknowledgement contains a unique identifier for each request and the initial status of the request and its validity. Clients can use this identifier to get the status of the execution of the flow. The figure below shows the structure of a DGL Data Grid Response.

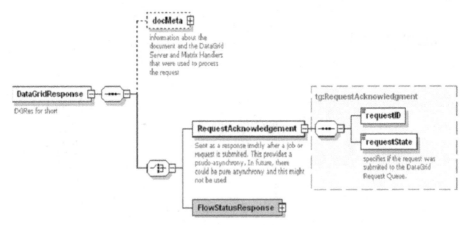

Fig. 4. Data Grid Response

Servicing Seismic and Oil Reservoir Simulation Data Through Grid Data Services*

Sivaramakrishnan Narayanan, Tahsin Kurc, Umit Catalyurek, and Joel Saltz

Department of Biomedical Informatics,
The Ohio State University, Columbus, OH, 43210
{krishnan, kurc, umit, jsaltz}@bmi.osu.edu

Abstract. This paper presents the implementation of a two layer infrastructure for servicing queries against large datasets generated in oil reservoir simulation studies in the Grid. The first layer implements *object-relational virtualization* of file-based dataset stored on a storage cluster. The second layer provides an implementation of Grid Data Services via Open Grid Services Architecture Data Access and Integration (OGSA-DAI) middleware.

1 Introduction

In an increasing number of engineering and science fields, the volume of data generated and processed is in the order of terabytes. Simulation-based oil reservoir management studies are an example of applications that generate and reference large volumes of simulation and experimental data. The objective is to develop complex numerical models of subsurface reservoirs and use these models to efficiently search for alternative oil production strategies in order to optimize profits and minimize adverse effects to the environment [20,28]. In this optimization process, there is a need to provide support for management and querying of large volumes of data, generated by simulations or collected from field measurements, in order to be able to refine model parameters and determine the next set of simulations to be carried out. In addition, the datasets can be generated and stored at multiple locations, since the computational requirements of the simulations may require use of machines at supercomputing centers.

There has been considerable progress in Grid computing technologies in recent years. In addition to a wide array of middleware systems and tools, a services-based view of the Grid has emerged. In this view, data sources and applications are exposed to the environment using standard interfaces. Users interact with the resources through well-defined Grid services protocols. In this way, the complexities and heterogeneity of individual resources can be hidden from clients and greater interoperability among applications can be achieved.

---

* This research was supported in part by the National Science Foundation under Grants #ACI-9619020 (UC Subcontract #10152408), #EIA-0121177, #ACI-0203846, #ACI-0130437, #ANI-0330612, #ACI-9982087, #CCF-0342615, #CNS-0406386, #CNS-0426241, Lawrence Livermore National Laboratory under Grant #B517095 (UC Subcontract #10184497), NIH NIBIB BISTI #P20EB000591, Ohio Board of Regents BRTTC #BRTT02-0003.

Several core functions need to be supported in an end-to-end system for enabling data-driven scientific applications in a Grid environment. These functions include management of data types and metadata, virtualization of data sources and data subsetting, data product generation (e.g., data aggregates from data subsets), and Grid services interfaces. In our work, we develop an integrated suite of middleware components to support these functions. These middleware components are shown in Figure 1. In this suite, DataCutter, which is a component-based middleware, enables combined use of task- and data-parallelism and is used to support data product generation (e.g., aggregates of data subsets) [7]; STORM [22,23] provides virtualization of file based datasets as object-relational tables and support for data subsetting; Mobius [19] supports management of data definitions and data types as XML schemas, XML virtualization of data, and metadata management. In an ongoing project, we are integrating these middleware systems with the Open Grid Services Architecture Data Access and Integration (OGSA-DAI) middleware toolkit [24] to allow access to the functionality provided by these components via OGSA-DAI Grid services protocols.

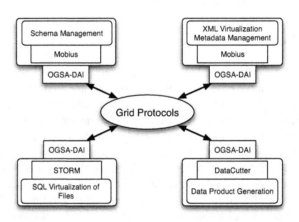

Fig. 1. Middleware components and toolkits to support data-driven scientific applications in the Grid

In this paper, we describe the design and implementation of a layered infrastructure for serving large, distributed datasets generated in oil reservoir simulation studies in a Grid environment using STORM and OGSA-DAI. The first layer in our infrastructure implements support for efficient use of distributed storage clusters and enables *object-relational virtualization* of file-based datasets. This layer builds on the STORM middleware framework. The second layer leverages the existing work in the Grid community to provide integrated access to datasets served by multiple STORM instances. This layer is implemented using the OGSA-DAI middleware toolkit. We describe the integration of STORM as a data source in OGSA-DAI and present a preliminary performance evaluation of the integrated system.

2   Oil Reservoir Management Studies

Effective oil reservoir management requires accurate characterization of the reservoir properties and efficient management strategies that involve optimized placement of production and injection wells. Simulation-based oil reservoir management is a viable approach to evaluate different optimization strategies and to understand changes in reservoir properties over long periods of time [20]. The main steps of this optimization process are shown in Figure 2. Various production strategies (i.e., the number of placement of injection and production wells) are simulated using a numerical model of the reservoir under study. In addition, changes in reservoir characteristics (e.g., rock properties) over time are tracked by seismic data simulations (or seismic measurements in the field). Data obtained from seismic and reservoir simulations are stored for analysis. The data analysis processes subsets of seismic simulation datasets and reservoir simulation datasets in order to generate summary data such as production rates over a time period, bypass oil regions in the reservoir, and rock properties in the reservoir. The results of the analysis can be used to refine the reservoir models, simulate new production strategies, and collect additional seismic data.

In this section we briefly describe the oil reservoir simulation and seismic data simulation applications, the characteristics of their datasets, and the types of queries executed by users.

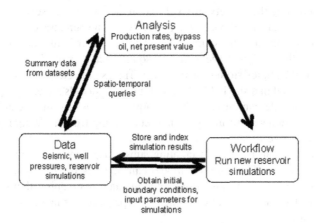

Fig. 2. Oil Reservoir Management

2.1   Oil Reservoir Simulation

A good understanding of fluid and rock properties in an oil reservoir is necessary for designing optimized production strategies. Since only a partial knowledge of critical parameters such as rock permeability in the reservoir is available, it is desirable to incorporate geologic uncertainty in complex reservoir models. An approach is to simulate alternative production strategies with varying number, type, timing and location of wells, applied to multiple realizations (simulation runs) of geostatistical models. This approach can lead to large volumes of output data [28].

Simulations are performed on a three-dimensional mesh over several time steps. Each realization corresponds to different geostatistical models and different number of wells and well placements. At each time step, the value of seventeen separate variables and cell locations in 3-dimensional space are output for each cell in the grid. Common analysis scenarios involve queries for economic evaluation as well as technical evaluation, such as determination of representative realizations and identification of areas of bypassed oil. Examples of client requests include *"Find all the potential bypassed oil cells between time T_1 and T_2 in realization A."* and *"Retrieve the oil saturation values at all mesh points from realizations A and B between time steps T_1 and T_2; visualize the results.".*

2.2   Seismic Data

The physical characteristics of a reservoir change over time. These changes in reservoir material properties should be detected and incorporated into reservoir models. Seismic surveys of the reservoir can be used to track changes [20]. Seismic data is recorded as sound traces generated by multiple sound sources on the surface and sampled by receivers at the bottom and on the surface of the reservoir. The sound traces are used to infer subsurface material properties. The surveys can be either carried out in the field or simulated using the seismic models of the reservoir.

A seismic dataset is stored in files in a standard exchange format, referred to as SEGY, defined by the Society of Exploration Geophysics. A seismic data file consists of a 3600-byte header followed by a record for each sound trace. Each record contains a 240-byte header and the sound trace. The header information stores the metadata associated with the sound trace including sound source id, receiver id, receiver location, the number of samples stored for the trace. Traces collected for a single sound source are usually stored in a single file. When numerical models are used to generate seismic data, each data file can be up to 25 Gigabytes in size and there can be thousands of data sources simulated, resulting in datasets ranging from a few terabytes to hundreds of terabytes in size.

Seismic data can be used in creating subsurface images and predicted subsurface material properties. The reservoir model can be revised by imaging and inversion of output from seismic data simulations. Imaging analysis requires that subsets of seismic data be selected based on, for example, the type of sensor in a recording array and for each or a suite of sources.

3   System Support

An end-to-end system to address the data management requirements of oil reservoir management studies in a Grid environment should provide a range of functions. The overall system architecture is illustrated in Figure 3. In this architecture, Mobius can be used to support management of metadata associated with simulation runs, seismic field measurements, and analysis results. The structure of data types can be managed by the Mobius schema management services. The support for data product generation (e.g., reconstruction of 3D volumes from seismic data, visualization of reservoir results) is provided by DataCutter. The STORM middleware can be used to support SQL-style select queries against large simulation datasets stored in distributed collection of files on a cluster of storage nodes. These components can be exposed to the Grid environment via OGSA-DAI service interfaces and can be accessed by clients using Grid Service protocols. In this section, we describe our implementation of the data subsetting support using STORM and OGSA-DAI.

Our goals are to enable efficient execution of data subsetting operations on large volumes of simulation data and to facilitate querying of datasets generated and maintained at multiple sites. To achieve this, some issues should be considered. First, datasets from engineering simulations are usually stored in files rather than in database management systems and files may have different formats. Second, storage requirements of datasets and computational cost of data subsetting operations on large data volumes could be very high. Finally, datasets should be made available to the community (Grid environment) using standard interfaces so that disparate user groups can interact with them in a unified way.

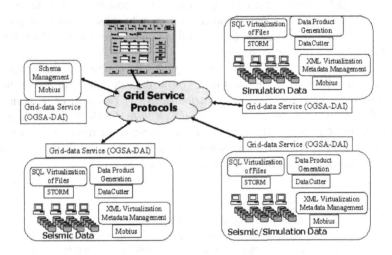

Fig. 3. A Grid-based Oil Reservoir Management System

In order to address these issues, we developed a layered architecture consisting of two interacting components. The first component addresses the first two issues by implementing a data virtualization layer at the data source and provides support for data subsetting operations on distributed and parallel storage clusters. The second component addresses the third issue by providing a Grid-services standardization layer and implements support for integration of datasets across multiple instances of the first component. We have built the first component on our STORM middleware framework. The second component leverages the OGSA-DAI infrastructure. Next, we briefly present an overview of STORM and OGSA-DAI followed by the description of implementation of the runtime support.

3.1 STORM

STORM [22,23] is a services-oriented framework designed to support processing of large datasets in a distributed environment. It provides basic database support for 1) *selection of the data of interest* from scientific datasets stored in files and 2) *transfer of selected data from storage nodes to compute nodes for processing*. The current implementation is based on a component infrastructure, called DataCutter [7], which supports distributed execution of networks of application-specific data processing components. Using the DataCutter runtime support, STORM can perform parallel I/O on distributed data and execute data selection and data filtering operations on heterogeneous collections of storage and compute clusters.

In order to support data subsetting on file-based datasets, STORM implements three abstractions: *virtual tables*, *select queries*, and *distributed arrays*. The first two abstractions are based on object-relational database models [31]. *SELECT* operation of the form shown in Figure 4 are supported on virtual tables. Data elements selected by the *SELECT* operation are grouped based on a computed attribute. In the figure, the $< Expression >$ statement can contain value-based selections and range queries. $Filter$ allows implementation of user-defined operations that are difficult to express with simple comparison operations.

The client program that carries out data processing can be a parallel program. In that case, the distribution among client nodes of the data elements returned as the result of the query can be represented as a *distributed array*. This abstraction is incorporated into the STORM framework by the *GROUP-BY-PROCESSOR* operation in the query formulation. $ComputeAttribute$ is another user-defined function that generates the attribute value on which the selected data elements are grouped together based on the application specific partitioning of data elements.

```
SELECT  < Data Elements >
        FROM  Dataset₁, Dataset₂, ..., Datasetₙ
        WHERE < Expression > AND < Filter(< Data Element >) >
        GROUP-BY-PROCESSOR ComputeAttribute(< Data Element >)
```

Fig. 4. Database queries supported by STORM

3.2 OGSA-DAI

The Grid has emerged as an integrated infrastructure for distributed computation [11,14]. The Open Grid Services Architecture (OGSA) [13] defines mechanisms for creating, managing, and exchanging information among entities called Grid services. The objective of the OGSA-DAI [24] initiative is to build upon the OGSA infrastructure to deliver high level data management functionality for the Grid. It defines services and interfaces that can be used by clients to specify operations on data resources and data. OGSA-DAI services can be configured and customized to expose a specific database management system.

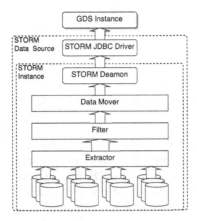

Fig. 5. Exposing STORM via OGSA-DAI

3.3 System Implementation

In STORM, in order to expose a new database, the application developer must provide implementations of two base interfaces: *Index* and *Extractor*. Relevant metadata associated with datasets should also be stored in the metadata services. In our implementation, metadata information associated with seismic dataset consists of the names of the data files that make up the dataset and the names of the data attributes, which include sound source id, receiver id, survey date, and source and receiver coordinates. A client can submit queries to the system on these attributes. Seismic datasets are stored as a set of files, each of which corresponds to sound traces collected from one or more sound sources. We implemented an extraction object which reads a record from the data file, extracts the dataset attributes from the header along with the trace data, and forms a tuple consisting of the attribute values and the trace data. We used an R-Tree [18] to index the dataset. We followed a similar implementation strategy for oil reservoir simulation datasets. A detailed description of the implementation can be found in [22].

The Grid Data Service (GDS) is the central OGSA-DAI component. OGSA-DAI provides default implementation of a Grid Data Service (GDS) that can expose databases that implement the JDBC interface. In order to take advantage of this, we have developed a JDBC driver implementation for STORM. This allows the default GDS implementation to use a standard interface to communicate with the STORM runtime. The JDBC driver also exposes the metadata corresponding to the tables (virtual tables) that the particular STORM instance serves.

When the GDS receives a *SELECT* query, it passes it on to the JDBC driver. The JDBC driver parses the query into the internal format used in STORM and sends it to the STORM daemon over a TCP/IP connection. Results are forwarded from STORM to GDS via the JDBC driver, which implements the ResultSet interface. The JDBC driver reads the results from STORM as a stream of bytes. It then parses the results into appropriate Java objects. Note that parsing objects may also require conversion from little endian to big endian format.

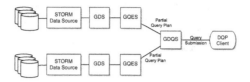

Fig. 6. Querying multiple data sources using DQP, OGSA-DAI, and STORM

With this setup, a STORM instance can be exposed as a data source as is shown Figure 5. A user wanting to submit a query over disparate data sources that are wrapped by OGSA-DAI GDSs can also use the Distribute Query Processing (DQP) infrastructure, which implements a distributed query engine on OGSA-DAI data sources [2]. Figure 6 illustrates an instance of querying multiple data sources using STORM, DQP, and OGSA-DAI layers.

It is possible that for some kind of queries, the JDBC driver of STORM may prove to be a bottleneck. We incorporated a feature wherein the driver can interpret the data it receives from the STORM daemon in different ways. For example, an 84 byte record consisting of 21 floats may be interpreted as a single 84 byte array. The intuition behind this is that it is less expensive to interpret a record as an array of bytes rather than parse them into individual Java objects. This notion can be further extended to interpret a sequence of records as a single larger record to reduce the number of operations performed per record. We should note that this approach, however, will remove interoperability with OGSA-DQP since the DQP requires knowledge of individual attributes to execute operations like *PROJECT* and *JOIN*.

4   Experimental Results

For the experimental evaluation, we used two PC clusters. The first one, called *mob*, consists of 8 nodes equipped with dual 1.4 GHz AMD Opteron processors, 8 GB of memory and 1.5 TB of disk storage in RAID 5 SATA disk arrays. The nodes are connected to each other via a Gigabit switch. The second cluster, called *xio*, consists of 16 nodes, each node having two Intel Xeon 2.4GHz processors with hyper threading, resulting in 4 virtual CPUs per node. Each node has 4GB of memory and is connected to a distinct 7.3TB FAStT600 disk array. A detailed discussion of this cluster's I/O architecture can be found in [8]. We were able to achieve a raw I/O bandwidth (i.e., just reading data from disk without any selection operations) of 2.69 GB/s using STORM on the 16 *xio* nodes.

4.1   Comparison with MySQL

OGSA-DAI provides a default Data Resource implementation for MySQL. In our first set of experiments, we carried out a preliminary performance comparison between STORM and MySQL and their OGSA-DAI implementations. We generated tables with 6 floating point attributes, one of which is a unique attribute idf. No indexes were built on the tables. Experiments were done on a single node in the *mob* cluster.

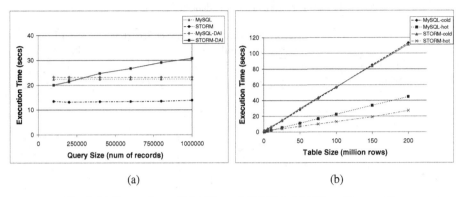

Fig. 7. (a) Comparison of MySQL and STORM. (b) Effect of large tables.

In Figure 7(a), we compare the performance of MySQL and STORM for vary-ing query sizes. Queries were of the form SELECT * FROM T100m WHERE idf < N where N corresponds exactly to the number of rows returned by the query. Here, T100m corresponds to a table with 100 million rows. We can see that STORM performs better than MySQL. Both systems take almost constant time to execute these queries because the scanning of the table takes up the bulk of the time. STORM's OGSA-DAI implementation is not as efficient as MySQL's, especially for very large queries. We attribute this to the fact that our current JDBC implementation is not well optimized. There is a high variable cost associated per tuple. However, STORM's implementa-tion outperforms MySQL for queries smaller than 300,000 records. This is because the fixed (startup) cost associated with STORM-DAI implementation is lower than that of the MySQL-DAI implementation.

We should note that there are time and space overheads associated with importing file-based data into a database. In our experiments, we observed that when data is im-ported to MySQL using by piping the binary files via hexdump utility and using the *LOAD DATA INFILE* command, the transfer time was about 600 seconds per GB of data.

Figure 7(b) highlights the effect of growing table sizes on a query's performance. Queries were of the form: SELECT * FROM TXm WHERE idf < 10000.0 where X is the size of the table in million rows. The cold-cache lines correspond to case when the filesystem's cache is purged by reading a large file. STORM and MySQL have al-most identical performance with the cold-cache. Our results show that I/O costs domi-nate the execution time in the cold-cache case. The hot-cache experiments were done by repeating the queries several times to allow for benefits of the filesystem's caching. In these experiments, STORM has a 40% improvement over MySQL, which we attribute to the lower per tuple processing cost of STORM.

4.2 Oil Reservoir Dataset

In these experiments, we used a 315 GB size oil reservoir dataset. This data corresponds to the simulation output of a single realization as described in Section 2.1. For every

Table 1. The characteristics of the datasets used in the experiments

Dataset	Attributes	Record Size (bytes)	Records (millions)	Dataset Size (GB)	Cluster Name Number of Nodes
Oil Reservoir	21	84	3,840	315	mob, 3
Seismic	16	4,240	247	1,056	xio, 16

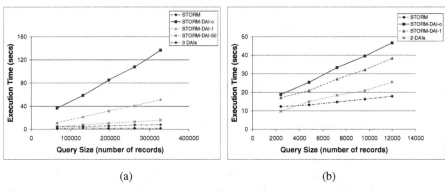

(a)   (b)

Fig. 8. (a) Varying query sizes on oil reservoir simulation data. (b) Performance on Seismic Data.

time step, each point of three-dimensional grid is stored as a tuple of 21 attributes; the values of seventeen separate variables, cell locations in 3-dimensional space and realization id. Simulation is done over a grid of size $512 \times 512 \times 256$ for 60 time steps (Table 1). The dataset is partitioned across 3 data nodes such that each node has roughly 1/3 of the dataset. The dataset is indexed using an R-Tree [18] on the X, Y, T, SOIL, VX attributes where X and Y are spatial attributes, T refers to the time step, SOIL is the saturation of oil at the grid location and VX is the velocity in the X direction.

Figure 8(a) shows the timing results with varying query size. The queries involve retrieving all data in a rectangular region over increasing intervals of time. The number of records retrieved, thus, grows linearly. Since the dataset is indexed, there is almost no excessive I/O and STORM takes about 2 seconds to execute these queries. The straight-forward method of exposing this dataset, denoted by *STORM-DAI-o* is very inefficient, due to parsing of 21 attributes in every record and creation of excessive number of Java objects. Combinig all 21 attributes into a single array (see Section 3.3), shown by the *STORM-DAI-1* line, results in a significant gain in performance. *STORM-DAI-50* combines 50 records into a single array which further improves performance. Combining larger number of records did not give us any further benefit. In Figure 8(a), *3 DAIs* shows the execution time when the dataset is distributed across three STORM-DAI-50 instances, each running on a single node. Each query was submitted to each STORM data source (i.e., the sub-tables) and the results were collected at the client. Partitioning the data across multiple data sources, improves parallelism among the STORM-DAI-50 instances resulting in better performance.

4.3   Seismic Dataset

To characterize STORM's performance on a single *xio* node, we considered a dataset with a single file of size 11 GB compliant with the SEGY format described in Section 2.2.

A base I/O rate of 193 MB/s was achieved using the *dd* unix utility on the *xio* node. As with any pipeline, bandwidth achieved increased with query size till a limiting value was reached. The bandwidth achieved at the end of the *Extractor* stage was 172 MB/s and at the end of the *Filtering* stage was 122 MB/s. The end-to-end bandwidth seen by the client was 55 MB/s. The memory-to-memory bandwidth, measured using the *memcpy* routine was about 560 MB/s. This was an important factor as communication between stages of the pipeline involves packing and unpacking tuples into/from buffers which involved a memory copy. Memory became the bottleneck that reduced the bandwidth at each stage of the pipeline. This is a problem in systems where the memory-to-memory bandwidth is comparable to I/O bandwidth. In our future work, we will investigate the option of changing pipeline depth at compile-time based on machine configuration.

In the next set of experiments, we used 96 seismic data files compliant with the SEGY file format described in Section 2.2. Each file contained traces for a single sound source, generated by a simulation using a seismic model of the reservoir and was 11 GB in size. Files were evenly distributed across the 16 nodes of the *xio* cluster. The dataset was indexed using an R-Tree on the RECV attribute that corresponds to the receiver number for a particular trace.

Queries returned all records that involved a certain set of receivers denoted by a range: SELECT * FROM segy WHERE RECV >= 1 AND RECV <= X where we varied X linearly. The results of this experiment are shown in Figure 8(b). The number of records returned by such a query is $96 * X$.

We employed similar techniques as in the previous experiments to improve the query execution performance. For these queries, STORM performs the same amount of I/O and filters out unwanted tuples. The fixed cost is therefore STORM's startup costs, the constant I/O and filtering costs. The variable cost is that of transferring the result of the filtering operations. We can see that the naive OGSA-DAI implementation has a high variable cost. Treating records as an array of bytes reduces this cost. Combining several records into a single array, however did not cause any improvements unlike in the oil reservoir experiments. This is because of the small number of rows returned by the query. To further improve performance we set up STORM and GDS instances on two nodes to serve half the table (each) and noticed a further improvement in performance. This is reflected in the *2-DAIs* line in the figure.

5   Related Work

Grid-technologies have been employed in several large-scale, multi-institutional projects in a wide range of science and engineering domains [4,9,10,17]. GriPhyN project [17] targets storage, cataloging and retrieval of large, measured datasets from large scale physical experiments. The goal is to deliver data products generated from these datasets to physicists across a wide-area network. The objective of Earth Systems Grid (ESG) project [9] is to provide Grid technologies for storage, publishing, and movement of large scale data from climate modeling applications. The EURO-GRID project [10] intends to develop tools for easy and seamless access to High Performance Computing (HPC) resources. The BioGrid component of the project implements the support for a uniform interface that will allow biologists and chemists to submit work to HPC facilities without having to worry about the details of running their work on different architectures. Biomedical Informatics Research Network (BIRN) (http://www.nbirn.net) [25] initiative focuses on support for collaborative access to and analysis of datasets generated by neuroimaging studies. The BIRN project uses the Storage Resource Broker (SRB) [26], which provides a distributed file system infrastructure, as a distributed data management middleware layer. MammoGrid [3] is a multi-institutional project funded by the Europen Union (EU). The objective of this project is to apply Grid middleware and tools to build a distributed database of mammograms and to investigate how it can be used to facilitate collaboration between researchers and clinicians across the EU. eDiamond [30] targets deployment of Grid infrastructure to manage, share, and analyze annotated mammograms captured and stored at multiple sites. One of the goals of MammoGrid and eDiamond is to develop and promote standardization in medical image databases for mammography and other cancer diseases. MEDIGRID [21,33] is another multi-institutionalproject investigating the application of Grid technologies for manipulating large medical image databases.

These large scale, multi-institutional projects share the same goal of deploying an infrastructure, building on Grid technologies, to facilitate sharing of data across institutions. In order to harness the collective power of distributed systems in a Grid environment, an array of tools and frameworks have been developed to support distributed storage, data replication, data processing, monitoring, security, and high-speed data transfers in Data and Computation Grids [16,15,26,35,7,1,32,34,6,19]. As Grid computing has become more ubiquitous, an Open Grid Services Architecture (OGSA) [12,13] has been proposed. There are some recent efforts to develop Grid and Web services implementations of database technologies. Raman et. al. [27] discusses a number of *virtualization* services to make data management and access transparent to Grid applications. These services provide support for access to distributed datasets, dynamic discovery of data sources, and collaboration. Bell et. al. [5] develop uniform web services interfaces, data and security models for relational databases. Smith et. al. [29] address the distributed execution of queries in a Grid environment. They describe an object-oriented database prototype running on MPICH-G and Globus.

6   Conclusion

We have presented a mechanism for integrated access to large scientific datasets. We have exposed STORM as a data resource and shown an example usage with the oil reservoir simulation and seismic data analysis applications and investigated the performance of the implementation. Our experiments show that the implementation scales well with query size and with number of data sources. As part of our future work, we will investigate the possibility of customizing the STORM pipeline based on machine configuration.

References

1. W. Allcock, A. Chervenak, I. Foster, C. Kesselman, C. Salisbury, and S. Tuecke. The Data Grid: Towards an architecture for the distributed management and analysis of large scientific datasets. *Journal of Network and Computer Applications*, 23:187–200, 2001.

2. M. Alpdemir, A. Mukherjee, A. Gounaris, N. W. Paton, P. Watson, and A. A. Fernandes. OGSA-DQP: A grid service for distributed querying on the grid. In *Proc. 9th International Conference on Extending Database Technology (EDBT)*, pages 858–861, 2004.

3. R. Amendolia, F. Estrella, T. Hauer, D. Manset, D. McCabe, R. McClatchey, M. Odeh, T. Reading, D. Rogulin, D. Schottlander, and T. Solomonides. Grid databases for shared image analysis in the mammogrid project. In *The Eighth International Database Engineering & Applications Symposium (Ideas'04)*, July 2004.

4. Asia Pacific BioGrid. http://www.apgrid.org.

5. W. H. Bell, D. Bosio, W. Hoschek, P. Kunszt, G. McCance, and M. Silander. Project spitfite - towards grid web service databases. http://www.cs.man.ac.uk/grid-db/documents.html.

6. F. Berman, A. Chien, K. Cooper, J. Dongarra, I. Foster, D. Gannon, L. Johnsson, K. Kennedy, C. Kesselman, J. Mellor-Crummey, D. Reed, L. Torczon, and R. Wolski. The GrADS Project: Software support for high-level Grid application development. *The International Journal of High Performance Computing Applications*, 15(4):327–344, Nov. 2001.

7. M. D. Beynon, T. Kurc, U. Catalyurek, C. Chang, A. Sussman, and J. Saltz. Distributed processing of very large datasets with DataCutter. *Parallel Computing*, 27(11):1457–1478, Oct. 2001.

8. S. Bokhari, B. Rutt, P. Wyckoff, and P. Buerger. An evaluation of the osc fastt600 turbo storage pool. Technical Report OSUBMI_TR_2004_n02, The Ohio State University, Department of Biomedical Informatics, Sep 2004.

9. Earth Systems Grid (ESG). http://www.earthsystemgrid.org.

10. EUROGRID. http://www.eurogrid.org/.

11. I. Foster and C. Kesselman. *The Grid: Blueprint for a New Computing Infrastructure*. Morgan Kaufmann Publishers, San Francisco, CA, USA, second edition, 2003.

12. I. Foster, C. Kesselman, J. Nick, and S. Tuecke. Grid services for distributed system integration. *IEEE Computer*, 36(6):37–46, June 2002.

13. I. Foster, C. Kesselman, J. M. Nick, and S. Tuecke. The physiology of the Grid: An Open Grid Services Architecture for distributed systems integration. *http://www.globus. org/research/papers/ogsa.pdf*, 2002.

14. I. Foster, C. Kesselman, and S. Tuecke. The anatomy of the Grid: Enabling scalable virtual organization. *The International Journal of High Performance Computing Applications*, 15(3):200–222, Fall 2001.

15. J. Frey, T. Tannenbaum, I. Foster, M. Livny, and S. Tuecke. Condor-G: A computation management agent for multi-institutional grids. In *Proceedings of the Tenth IEEE Symposium on High Performance Distributed Computing (HPDC10)*. IEEE Press, Aug 2001.

16. The Globus Project. http://www.globus.org.

17. Grid Physics Network (GriPhyN). http://www.griphyn.org.

18. A. Guttman. R-trees: A dynamic index structure for spatial searching. In *Proceedings of SIGMOD'84*, pages 47–57. ACM Press, May 1984.

19. S. Hastings, S. Langella, S. Oster, and J. Saltz. Distributed data management and integration: The mobius project. In *GGF Semantic Grid Workshop 2004*, pages 20–38. GGF, June 2004.

20. T. Kurc, U. Catalyurek, X. Zhang, J. Saltz, R. Martino, M. Wheeler, M. Peszyńska, A. Sussman, C. Hansen, M. Sen, R. Seifoullaev, P. Stoffa, C. Torres-Verdin, and M. Parashar. A simulation and data analysis system for large scale, data-driven oil reservoir simulation studies. *Concurrency and Computation: Practice and Experience. To appear.*, 2005.

21. J. Montagnat, V. Breton, and I. E. Magnin. Using grid technologies to face medical image analysis challenges. In *BioGrid'03, The 3rd International Symposium on Cluster Computing and the Grid (CCGrid 2003)*, pages 588–593, May 2003.
22. S. Narayanan, U. Catalyurek, T. Kurc, X. Zhang, and J. Saltz. Applying database support for large scale data driven science in distributed environments. In *Proceedings of the Fourth International Workshop on Grid Computing (Grid 2003)*, pages 141–148, Phoenix, Arizona, Nov 2003.
23. S. Narayanan, T. Kurc, U. Catalyurek, and J. Saltz. Database support for data-driven scientific applications in the grid. *Parallel Processing Letters*, 13(2):245–271, 2003.
24. Open Grid Services Architecture Data Access and Integration (OGSA-DAI). http://www.ogsadai.org.uk.
25. S. Peltier and M. Ellisman. *The Biomedical Informatics Research Network, in* The Grid, Blueprint for a New Computing Infrastructure. 2nd Edition: Elsevier, 2003.
26. A. Rajasekar, M. Wan, and R. Moore. MySRB & SRB - components of a data grid. In *The 11th International Symposium on High Performance Distributed Computing (HPDC-11)*, July 2002.
27. V. Raman, I. Narang, C. Crone, L. Haas, S. Malaika, T. Mukai, D. Wolfson, and C. Baru. Data access and management services on grid. http://www.cs.man.ac.uk/grid-db/documents.html.
28. J. Saltz, U. Catalyurek, T. Kurc, M. Gray, S. Hastings, S. Langella, S. Narayanan, R. Martino, S. Bryant, M. Peszynska, M. Wheeler, A. Sussman, M. Beynon, C. Hansen, D. Stredney, and D. Sessama. Driving scientific applications by data in distributed environments. In *Proceedings of Workshop on Dynamic Data Driven Application Systems (International Conference on Computational Science)*. Springer-Verlag, June 2003.
29. J. Smith, A. Gounaris, P. Watson, N. W. Paton, A. A. Fernandes, and R. Sakellariou. Distributed query processing on the grid. http://www.cs.man.ac.uk/grid-db/documents.html.
30. A. Solomonides, R. McClatchey, M. Odeh, M. Brady, M. Mulet-Parada, D. Schottlander, and S. Amendolia. Mammogrid and ediamond: Grids applications in mammogram analysis. In *Proceedings of the IADIS International Conference: e-Society 2003*, pages 1032–1033, 2003.
31. M. Stonebraker and P. Brown. *Object-Relational DBMSs, Tracking the Next Great Wave*. Morgan Kaufman Publishers, Inc., 1998.
32. D. Thain, J. Basney, S. Son, and M. Livny. Kangaroo approach to data movement on the grid. In *Proceedings of the Tenth IEEE Symposium on High Performance Distributed Computing (HPDC10)*, 2001.
33. T. Tweed and S. Miguet. Medical image database on the grid: Strategies for data distribution. In *HealthGrid'03*, pages 152–162, Jan. 2003.
34. S. Vazhkudai, S. Tuecke, and I. Foster. Replica selection in the globus data grid. In *International Workshop on Data Models and Databases on Clusters and the Grid (DataGrid 2001)*. IEEE Computer Society Press, 2001.
35. R. Wolski, N. Spring, and J. Hayes. The network weather service: A distributed resource performance forecasting service for metacomputing. *Journal of Future Generation Computing Systems*, 15(5-6):757–768, 1999.

Author Index

Antonioletti, Mario   71

Catalyurek, Umit   129
Comito, Carmela   4

da Silva, Vinícius F.V.   45
Ding, Allen   113
Dutra, Márcio L.   45

Fernandes, Alvaro A.A.   30
Fomkin, Ruslan   58

Gilbert, Lucas   113
Göres, Jürgen   16
Gounaris, Anastasios   30

Jagatheesan, Arun   113

Krause, Amy   71
Kuramoto, Jeffrey   113
Kurc, Tahsin   129

Mathew, Reena   113
Moore, Daniel   113
Moore, Reagan W.   1, 113

Narayanan, Sivaramakrishnan   129

Otoo, Ekow   85

Paton, Norman W.   30, 71
Porto, Fabio   45

Risch, Tore   58
Romosan, Alexandru   85
Rotem, Doron   85

Sakellariou, Rizos   30
Saltz, Joel   129
Schulze, Bruno   45
Seshadri, Sridhar   85
Shoshani, Arie   100
Sim, Alex   100
Smith, Jim   30
Stockinger, Kurt   100

Talia, Domenico   4
Tran, Mark   113

Vandekieft, Erik   113

Watson, Paul   30
Weinberg, Jonathan   113

Lecture Notes in Computer Science

For information about Vols. 1–3754

please contact your bookseller or Springer

Vol. 3860: D. Pointcheval (Ed.), Topics in Cryptology – CT-RSA 2006. XI, 365 pages. 2006.

Vol. 3855: E. A. Emerson, K.S. Namjoshi (Eds.), Verification, Model Checking, and Abstract Interpretation. XI, 443 pages. 2006.

Vol. 3850: R. Freund, G. Păun, G. Rozenberg, A. Salomaa (Eds.), Membrane Computing. IX, 371 pages. 2006.

Vol. 3842: H.T. Shen, J. Li, M. Li, J. Ni, W. Wang (Eds.), Advanced Web and Network Technologies, and Applications. XXVII, 1057 pages. 2005.

Vol. 3840: M. Li, B. Boehm, L.J. Osterweil (Eds.), Unifying the Software Process Spectrum. XVI, 522 pages. 2006.

Vol. 3838: A. Middeldorp, V. van Oostrom, F. van Raamsdonk, R. de Vrijer (Eds.), Processes, Terms and Cycles: Steps on the Road to Infinity. XVIII, 639 pages. 2005.

Vol. 3837: K. Cho, P. Jacquet (Eds.), Technologies for Advanced Heterogeneous Networks. IX, 307 pages. 2005.

Vol. 3836: J.-M. Pierson (Ed.), Data Management in Grids. X, 143 pages. 2005.

Vol. 3835: G. Sutcliffe, A. Voronkov (Eds.), Logic for Programming, Artificial Intelligence, and Reasoning. XIV, 744 pages. 2005. (Sublibrary LNAI).

Vol. 3834: D. Feitelson, E. Frachtenberg, L. Rudolph, U. Schwiegelshohn (Eds.), Job Scheduling Strategies for Parallel Processing. VIII, 283 pages. 2005.

Vol. 3833: K.-J. Li, C. Vangenot (Eds.), Web and Wireless Geographical Information Systems. XI, 309 pages. 2005.

Vol. 3832: D. Zhang, A.K. Jain (Eds.), Advances in Biometrics. XX, 796 pages. 2005.

Vol. 3831: J. Wiedermann, G. Tel, J. Pokorný, M. Bieliková, J. Štuller (Eds.), SOFSEM 2006: Theory and Practice of Computer Science. XV, 576 pages. 2006.

Vol. 3829: P. Pettersson, W. Yi (Eds.), Formal Modeling and Analysis of Timed Systems. IX, 305 pages. 2005.

Vol. 3828: X. Deng, Y. Ye (Eds.), Internet and Network Economics. XVII, 1106 pages. 2005.

Vol. 3827: X. Deng, D. Du (Eds.), Algorithms and Computation. XX, 1190 pages. 2005.

Vol. 3826: B. Benatallah, F. Casati, P. Traverso (Eds.), Service-Oriented Computing - ICSOC 2005. XVIII, 597 pages. 2005.

Vol. 3824: L.T. Yang, M. Amamiya, Z. Liu, M. Guo, F.J. Rammig (Eds.), Embedded and Ubiquitous Computing – EUC 2005. XXIII, 1204 pages. 2005.

Vol. 3823: T. Enokido, L. Yan, B. Xiao, D. Kim, Y. Dai, L.T. Yang (Eds.), Embedded and Ubiquitous Computing – EUC 2005 Workshops. XXXII, 1317 pages. 2005.

Vol. 3822: D. Feng, D. Lin, M. Yung (Eds.), Information Security and Cryptology. XII, 420 pages. 2005.

Vol. 3821: R. Ramanujam, S. Sen (Eds.), FSTTCS 2005: Foundations of Software Technology and Theoretical Computer Science. XIV, 566 pages. 2005.

Vol. 3820: L.T. Yang, X. Zhou, W. Zhao, Z. Wu, Y. Zhu, M. Lin (Eds.), Embedded Software and Systems. XXVIII, 779 pages. 2005.

Vol. 3819: P. Van Hentenryck (Ed.), Practical Aspects of Declarative Languages. X, 231 pages. 2005.

Vol. 3818: S. Grumbach, L. Sui, V. Vianu (Eds.), Advances in Computer Science – ASIAN 2005. XIII, 294 pages. 2005.

Vol. 3816: G. Chakraborty (Ed.), Distributed Computing and Internet Technology. XXI, 606 pages. 2005.

Vol. 3815: E.A. Fox, E.J. Neuhold, P. Premsmit, V. Wuwongse (Eds.), Digital Libraries: Implementing Strategies and Sharing Experiences. XVII, 529 pages. 2005.

Vol. 3814: M. Maybury, O. Stock, W. Wahlster (Eds.), Intelligent Technologies for Interactive Entertainment. XV, 342 pages. 2005. (Sublibrary LNAI).

Vol. 3813: R. Molva, G. Tsudik, D. Westhoff (Eds.), Security and Privacy in Ad-hoc and Sensor Networks. VIII, 219 pages. 2005.

Vol. 3810: Y.G. Desmedt, H. Wang, Y. Mu, Y. Li (Eds.), Cryptology and Network Security. XI, 349 pages. 2005.

Vol. 3809: S. Zhang, R. Jarvis (Eds.), AI 2005: Advances in Artificial Intelligence. XXVII, 1344 pages. 2005. (Sublibrary LNAI).

Vol. 3808: C. Bento, A. Cardoso, G. Dias (Eds.), Progress in Artificial Intelligence. XVIII, 704 pages. 2005. (Sublibrary LNAI).

Vol. 3807: M. Dean, Y. Guo, W. Jun, R. Kaschek, S. Krishnaswamy, Z. Pan, Q.Z. Sheng (Eds.), Web Information Systems Engineering – WISE 2005 Workshops. XV, 275 pages. 2005.

Vol. 3806: A.H. H. Ngu, M. Kitsuregawa, E.J. Neuhold, J.-Y. Chung, Q.Z. Sheng (Eds.), Web Information Systems Engineering – WISE 2005. XXI, 771 pages. 2005.

Vol. 3805: G. Subsol (Ed.), Virtual Storytelling. XII, 289 pages. 2005.

Vol. 3804: G. Bebis, R. Boyle, D. Koracin, B. Parvin (Eds.), Advances in Visual Computing. XX, 755 pages. 2005.

Vol. 3803: S. Jajodia, C. Mazumdar (Eds.), Information Systems Security. XI, 342 pages. 2005.

Vol. 3802: Y. Hao, J. Liu, Y.-P. Wang, Y.-m. Cheung, H. Yin, L. Jiao, J. Ma, Y.-C. Jiao (Eds.), Computational Intelligence and Security, Part II. XLII, 1166 pages. 2005. (Sublibrary LNAI).

Vol. 3801: Y. Hao, J. Liu, Y.-P. Wang, Y.-m. Cheung, H. Yin, L. Jiao, J. Ma, Y.-C. Jiao (Eds.), Computational Intelligence and Security, Part I. XLI, 1122 pages. 2005. (Sublibrary LNAI).

Vol. 3799: M. A. Rodríguez, I.F. Cruz, S. Levashkin, M.J. Egenhofer (Eds.), GeoSpatial Semantics. X, 259 pages. 2005.

Vol. 3798: A. Dearle, S. Eisenbach (Eds.), Component Deployment. X, 197 pages. 2005.

Vol. 3797: S. Maitra, C. E. V. Madhavan, R. Venkatesan (Eds.), Progress in Cryptology - INDOCRYPT 2005. XIV, 417 pages. 2005.

Vol. 3796: N.P. Smart (Ed.), Cryptography and Coding. XI, 461 pages. 2005.

Vol. 3795: H. Zhuge, G.C. Fox (Eds.), Grid and Cooperative Computing - GCC 2005. XXI, 1203 pages. 2005.

Vol. 3794: X. Jia, J. Wu, Y. He (Eds.), Mobile Ad-hoc and Sensor Networks. XX, 1136 pages. 2005.

Vol. 3793: T. Conte, N. Navarro, W.-m.W. Hwu, M. Valero, T. Ungerer (Eds.), High Performance Embedded Architectures and Compilers. XIII, 317 pages. 2005.

Vol. 3792: I. Richardson, P. Abrahamsson, R. Messnarz (Eds.), Software Process Improvement. VIII, 215 pages. 2005.

Vol. 3791: A. Adi, S. Stoutenburg, S. Tabet (Eds.), Rules and Rule Markup Languages for the Semantic Web. X, 225 pages. 2005.

Vol. 3790: G. Alonso (Ed.), Middleware 2005. XIII, 443 pages. 2005.

Vol. 3789: A. Gelbukh, Á. de Albornoz, H. Terashima-Marín (Eds.), MICAI 2005: Advances in Artificial Intelligence. XXVI, 1198 pages. 2005. (Sublibrary LNAI).

Vol. 3788: B. Roy (Ed.), Advances in Cryptology - ASIACRYPT 2005. XIV, 703 pages. 2005.

Vol. 3787: D. Kratsch (Ed.), Graph-Theoretic Concepts in Computer Science. XIV, 470 pages. 2005.

Vol. 3785: K.-K. Lau, R. Banach (Eds.), Formal Methods and Software Engineering. XIV, 496 pages. 2005.

Vol. 3784: J. Tao, T. Tan, R.W. Picard (Eds.), Affective Computing and Intelligent Interaction. XIX, 1008 pages. 2005.

Vol. 3783: S. Qing, W. Mao, J. Lopez, G. Wang (Eds.), Information and Communications Security. XIV, 492 pages. 2005.

Vol. 3782: K.-D. Althoff, A. Dengel, R. Bergmann, M. Nick, T. Roth-Berghofer (Eds.), Professional Knowledge Management. XXIII, 739 pages. 2005. (Sublibrary LNAI).

Vol. 3781: S.Z. Li, Z. Sun, T. Tan, S. Pankanti, G. Chollet, D. Zhang (Eds.), Advances in Biometric Person Authentication. XI, 250 pages. 2005.

Vol. 3780: K. Yi (Ed.), Programming Languages and Systems. XI, 435 pages. 2005.

Vol. 3779: H. Jin, D. Reed, W. Jiang (Eds.), Network and Parallel Computing. XV, 513 pages. 2005.

Vol. 3778: C. Atkinson, C. Bunse, H.-G. Gross, C. Peper (Eds.), Component-Based Software Development for Embedded Systems. VIII, 345 pages. 2005.

Vol. 3777: O.B. Lupanov, O.M. Kasim-Zade, A.V. Chaskin, K. Steinhöfel (Eds.), Stochastic Algorithms: Foundations and Applications. VIII, 239 pages. 2005.

Vol. 3776: S.K. Pal, S. Bandyopadhyay, S. Biswas (Eds.), Pattern Recognition and Machine Intelligence. XXIV, 808 pages. 2005.

Vol. 3775: J. Schönwälder, J. Serrat (Eds.), Ambient Networks. XIII, 281 pages. 2005.

Vol. 3774: G. Bierman, C. Koch (Eds.), Database Programming Languages. X, 295 pages. 2005.

Vol. 3773: A. Sanfeliu, M.L. Cortés (Eds.), Progress in Pattern Recognition, Image Analysis and Applications. XX, 1094 pages. 2005.

Vol. 3772: M.P. Consens, G. Navarro (Eds.), String Processing and Information Retrieval. XIV, 406 pages. 2005.

Vol. 3771: J.M.T. Romijn, G.P. Smith, J. van de Pol (Eds.), Integrated Formal Methods. XI, 407 pages. 2005.

Vol. 3770: J. Akoka, S.W. Liddle, I.-Y. Song, M. Bertolotto, I. Comyn-Wattiau, W.-J. van den Heuvel, M. Kolp, J. Trujillo, C. Kop, H.C. Mayr (Eds.), Perspectives in Conceptual Modeling. XXII, 476 pages. 2005.

Vol. 3769: D.A. Bader, M. Parashar, V. Sridhar, V.K. Prasanna (Eds.), High Performance Computing – HiPC 2005. XXVIII, 550 pages. 2005.

Vol. 3768: Y.-S. Ho, H.J. Kim (Eds.), Advances in Multimedia Information Processing - PCM 2005, Part II. XXVIII, 1088 pages. 2005.

Vol. 3767: Y.-S. Ho, H.J. Kim (Eds.), Advances in Multimedia Information Processing - PCM 2005, Part I. XXVIII, 1022 pages. 2005.

Vol. 3766: N. Sebe, M.S. Lew, T.S. Huang (Eds.), Computer Vision in Human-Computer Interaction. X, 231 pages. 2005.

Vol. 3765: Y. Liu, T. Jiang, C. Zhang (Eds.), Computer Vision for Biomedical Image Applications. X, 563 pages. 2005.

Vol. 3764: S. Tixeuil, T. Herman (Eds.), Self-Stabilizing Systems. VIII, 229 pages. 2005.

Vol. 3762: R. Meersman, Z. Tari, P. Herrero (Eds.), On the Move to Meaningful Internet Systems 2005: OTM 2005 Workshops. XXXI, 1228 pages. 2005.

Vol. 3761: R. Meersman, Z. Tari (Eds.), On the Move to Meaningful Internet Systems 2005: CoopIS, DOA, and ODBASE, Part II. XXVII, 653 pages. 2005.

Vol. 3760: R. Meersman, Z. Tari (Eds.), On the Move to Meaningful Internet Systems 2005: CoopIS, DOA, and ODBASE, Part I. XXVII, 921 pages. 2005.

Vol. 3759: G. Chen, Y. Pan, M. Guo, J. Lu (Eds.), Parallel and Distributed Processing and Applications - ISPA 2005 Workshops. XIII, 669 pages. 2005.

Vol. 3758: Y. Pan, D.-x. Chen, M. Guo, J. Cao, J.J. Dongarra (Eds.), Parallel and Distributed Processing and Applications. XXIII, 1162 pages. 2005.

Vol. 3757: A. Rangarajan, B. Vemuri, A.L. Yuille (Eds.), Energy Minimization Methods in Computer Vision and Pattern Recognition. XII, 666 pages. 2005.

Vol. 3756: J. Cao, W. Nejdl, M. Xu (Eds.), Advanced Parallel Processing Technologies. XIV, 526 pages. 2005.